TURBO C®

THE POCKET REFERENCE

Herbert Schildt

Osborne **McGraw-Hill**
Berkeley, California

Osborne **McGraw-Hill**
2600 Tenth Street
Berkeley, California 94710
U.S.A.

For information on translations and book distributors outside of the U.S.A., please write to Osborne **McGraw-Hill** at the above address.

Turbo C® : The Pocket Reference

1234567890 DODO 898

ISBN 0-07-881381-6

Copy Editor: Barbara Conway
Word Processor: Bonnie Bozorg
Proofreader: Kay Luthin
Production Supervisor: Kevin Shafer

CONTENTS

Quite a few Turbo C structure definitions have been presented and discussed in this book. The definitions originate in the Turbo C manuals and disk files. These structure definitions are used with permission from Borland International, Inc., developer of Turbo C.

INTRODUCTION

Turbo C is the latest torch bearer of a proud tradition. With virtually no organized support, the C language has gone from relative obscurity to international acclaim in a little over a decade. It is the language of choice for most professional programmers.

C was invented and first implemented by Dennis Ritchie on a DEC PDP-11 using the UNIX operating system. C is the result of a development process that started with an older language called BCPL, which is still in use (primarily in Europe) and was developed by Martin Richards. BCPL influenced a language called B, invented by Ken Thompson, which led to the development of C.

For many years, the de facto standard for C was the one supplied with the UNIX version 5 operating system and described in *The C Programming Language* by Brian Kernighan and Dennis Ritchie (Prentice-Hall, 1978). It is often referred to as the "K&R standard."

With the popularity of microcomputers, a large number of C implementations were created. In what could almost be called a miracle, most of these implementations were highly compatible with each other on the source code level. However, because no standard existed, there were discrepancies. To alter this situation, a committee was established in 1983 to start work on the creation of an ANSI standard that would define the C language once and for all. As of this writing, the proposed standard is very near completion. Turbo C fully supports the proposed ANSI standard.

OPERATORS

C has a very rich set of operators that can be divided into the following classes: arithmetic, relational and logical, bitwise, pointer, assignment, and miscellaneous.

Arithmetic Operators

C has the following seven arithmetic operators:

Operator	**Action**
-	Subtraction, unary minus
+	Addition
*	Multiplication
/	Division
%	Modulo division
--	Decrement
++	Increment

The +, -, *, and / operators work as expected. The % operator returns the remainder of an integer division. The increment and decrement operators increase or decrease the operand by one.

The precedence of these operators is as follows:

highest	++
	--
	- (unary minus)
	*
	/
	%

+

lowest -

Operators on the same precedence level are evaluated from left to right.

Relational and Logical Operators

The relational and logical operators are used to produce TRUE/FALSE results and are often used together. In C, any nonzero number evaluates as TRUE. However, a C relational or logical expression produces the number 1 for TRUE and 0 for FALSE. The relational and logical operators are listed here:

Relational Operator	Meaning
	Greater than
=	Greater than or equal
<	Less than
<=	Less than or equal
==	Equal
!=	Not equal

<table>
<tr><th>Logical Operator</th><th>Meaning</th></tr>
<tr><td>&&</td><td>AND</td></tr>
<tr><td>||</td><td>OR</td></tr>
<tr><td>!</td><td>NOT</td></tr>
</table>

The relational operators are used to compare two values. The logical operators are used to connect two values or, in the case of NOT, to reverse the value of a value. The precedence of these operators is

highest	!
	=
	<
	<=
	==
	!
	==
	&&
lowest	||

As an example, the following **if** statement evaluates TRUE and prints the line **X is less than 10**:

```
X = 9;
if(X < 10) printf("X is less than 10");
```

In the following example, however, no message is displayed, because both operands associated with AND must be true for the outcome to be true:

```
X = 9;
Y = 9;
if(X < 10 && Y > 10) printf("X is less than 10; Y is
greater");
```

The Bitwise Operators

Unlike most other programming languages, C provides operators that manipulate the actual bits inside a variable. The bitwise operators listed here can be used only on integers or characters.

<table>
<tr><th>Bitwise
Operator</th><th>Meaning</th></tr>
<tr><td>&</td><td>AND</td></tr>
<tr><td>|</td><td>OR</td></tr>
<tr><td>^</td><td>XOR</td></tr>
<tr><td>~</td><td>One's complement</td></tr>
<tr><td>></td><td>Right shift</td></tr>
<tr><td><<</td><td>Left shift</td></tr>
</table>

AND, OR, and XOR The truth tables for AND, OR, and XOR are as follows:

&	0	1
0	0	0
1	0	1

1	0	1
0	0	1
1	1	1

^	0	1
0	0	1
1	1	0

These rules are applied to each bit in a byte when the bitwise operations AND, OR, and XOR are performed. Here are some examples:

```
 0100 1101
&0011 1011
----------
 0000 1001

 0100 1101
|0011 1011
----------
 0111 1111

 0100 1101
^0011 1011
----------
 0111 0110
```

In a program, you use &, |, and ^ like any other operators, as shown here:

```
main()
{
  char x,y,z;

  x = 1; y = 2; z = 4;
  x = x & y; /* x now equals zero */

  y = x | z; /* y now equals 4 */

}
```

The One's Complement Operator The one's complement operator, ~, will invert all the bits in a byte. For example, if a character variable **ch** has the bit pattern

```
0011 1001
```

then

```
ch = ~ch;
```

places the following bit pattern into **ch**:

```
1100 0110
```

The Shift Operators The right and left shift operators shift all bits in a byte or a word a specified amount. As bits are shifted, zeros are brought in. The number on the right side of the shift operator specifies the number of positions to shift. The general form of each shift operator is

```
variable >> number of bit positions

variable << number of bit positions
```

Given the bit pattern

```
0011 1101
```

a shift right yields

```
0001 1110
```

while a shift left produces

```
0111 1010
```

A shift right is effectively a division by 2, and a shift left is a multiplication by 2. The following code fragment will first multiply and then divide the value in **x**:

```
int x;

x = 10;
x = x<<1;
x = x>>1;
```

Because of the way negative numbers are represented inside the machine, you must be careful if you try to use a shift for multiplication or division. Moving a 1 into the most significant bit position will make the computer think that it is dealing with a negative number.

The precedence of the bitwise operators is

highest	~
	<<
	&
	^
lowest	|

Pointer Operators

The two pointer operators are * and &. It is unfortunate that these operators use the same symbols as the multiplication operator and the bitwise AND, because they have nothing in common with them.

The & Pointer Operator The & operator returns the address of the variable it precedes. For example, if the integer **x** is located at memory address 1000, then

```
y = &x;
```

places the value 1000 into **y**. The & operator can be thought of as "the address of." For example, the previous statement could be read as "place the address of x into y."

The * Pointer Operator The * operator uses the value of the variable it precedes as the address of a variable in memory. For example,

```
y = &x;

*y = 100;
```

places the value 100 into **x**. The * can be remembered as "at address." In this example, it could be read as "place the value 100 at address y." The * operator can also be used on the right-hand side of an assignment. For example,

```
y = &x;

*y = 100;

z = *y/10;
```

places the value of 10 into **z**.

void Pointers A pointer of type **void** is said to be a generic pointer that can be used to point to any type of object. This implies that pointers of any type can be assigned to pointers of type **void**, and vice versa, by using the appropriate type-casts. To declare a **void** pointer you use a declaration similar to the one shown here:

```
void *p;
```

The **void** pointer is particulary useful when various types of pointers will be manipulated by a single routine.

Assignment Operators

In C, the assignment operator is the single equal sign. However, C allows a very convenient form of shorthand for assignments of this general type:

```
variable1 = variable1 operator expression;
```

For example, assignments of the type

```
x = x+10;

y = y/z;
```

can be shortened to

```
variable1 operator = expression;
```

Thus, the two example expressions can be shortened to

```
x += 10;

y /= z;
```

The ? Operator

The ? operator is a ternary operator that is used to replace **if** statements of the general type

```
if expression1 then x=expression2
  else x=expression3
```

The general form of the ? operator is

```
variable = expression1 ? expression2 : expression3;
```

If expression1 is TRUE, then the value assigned is that of expression2; otherwise, it is the value of expression3. For example,

```
x = (y<10) ? 20 : 40;
```

will assign **x** the value of 20 if **y** is less than 10 and 40 if it is not less than 10.

Structure and Union Operators

The . (dot) operator and the -> (arrow) operator are used to reference individual elements of structures and unions. The dot operator is applied to the actual structure or union. The arrow operator is used with a pointer to a structure or a union. For example, given the global structure

```
struct date_time {
  char date[16];
  int time;
} tm;
```

to assign the value 3/12/88 to element **date** of structure **tm**, you would write

```
strcpy(tm->date, "3/12/88");
```

However, if **p_tm** is a pointer to a structure of type **date_time**, then the following statement is used:

```
strcpy(tm->date, "3/12/88");
```

The Comma Operator

The comma operator is used primarily in the **for** statement to cause a sequence of operations to be performed. When it is used on the right side of an assignment statement, the value of the entire expression is the value of the last expression of the comma-separated list. For example, when

```
y = 10;

x = (y-=5, 100/y);
```

is executed, **x** will have the value 20 because **y**'s original value of 10 is reduced by 5, and then that value is divided into 100, yielding 20 as the result. You can think of the comma operator as meaning "do this and this" and so on.

sizeof

Although **sizeof** is a keyword, it is also a compile-time operator used to determine the size, in bytes, of a variable or data type, including user-defined structures and unions. If used with a type, the type name must be enclosed by parentheses.

This example prints the number 2:

```
int x;

printf("%d", sizeof (x);
```

The Cast

A *cast* is a special operator that forces one data type to be converted into another. The general form is

```
(type) variable
```

For example, for the integer **count** to be used in a call to **sqrt()**, the Turbo C Standard Library square root routine that requires a floating point parameter, a cast is used to force **count** to be treated as type **double**:

```
double y;
int count;

count = 10;

y = sqrt((double)count);
```

Operator Precedence Summary

The precedence of all C operators is listed here. Note that all operators, except the unary operators and ?, associate from left to right. The unary operators, *, &, -, and the ? operator associate from right to left.

highest (cast) [] -> .
! ~ ++ -- - (type) * & **sizeof**
* / %
+ -
<< >>
< <= > >=
== !=
&
^
|
&&
||
?:
= += -= *= /= %= >>= <<= &= ^= |=
lowest ,

KEYWORD SUMMARY

As defined by the proposed ANSI standard, the following are the 32 keywords that, combined with the formal C syntax, form the C language:

auto	**double**	**int**	**struct**
break	**else**	**long**	**switch**
case	**enum**	**register**	**typedef**
char	**extern**	**return**	**union**
const	**float**	**short**	**unsigned**
continue	**for**	**signed**	**void**
default	**goto**	**sizeof**	**volatile**
do	**if**	**static**	**while**

In addition to these Turbo C has added the following keywords to allow greater control over the way memory and other system resources are used:

_cs	**_ds**	**_es**	**_ss**
cdecl	**far**	**huge**	**interrupt**
near	**pascal**		

All C keywords are lowercase. C differentiates between uppercase and lowercase; therefore, **else** is a keyword, but ELSE is not.

Here is a brief synopsis of the Turbo C keywords.

auto The **auto** keyword is used to make temporary variables that are created when entering a block and destroyed when exiting. Consider this program:

```
main()
{
  for(;;) {
    if(getche()=='a') {
      auto int t;
      for(t=0; t<'a'; t++)
        printf("%d ", t);
    }
  }
}
```

In this example, the variable **t** is created only if the user types an "a". Outside of the **if** block, **t** is completely unknown, and any reference to it would generate a compile-time syntax error.

break The **break** keyword is used to exit from a **do, for,** or **while** loop, bypassing the normal loop condition. It is also used to exit from a **switch** statement.

Here is an example of **break** in a loop:

```
while(x<100) {
  x = get_new_x();
  if(keystroke()) break; /* key hit on keyboard */
  process(x);

}
```

Here, if a key is typed, the loop will terminate no matter what the value of **x** is.

A **break** always terminates the innermost **for, do, while,** or **switch** statement, regardless of the way these might be nested. In a **switch** statement, **break** effectively keeps program execution from "falling through" to the next **case** (see the discussion of the **switch** statement for details).

case See the discussion of the **switch** statement.

char The **char** data type specifier is used to declare character variables.

cdecl The **cdecl** keyword is not part of the ANSI standard. It forces Turbo C to compile a function so that its parameter passing conforms with the standard C calling convention. This keyword is used when you are compiling an entire file with the Pascal option and you want a specific function to be compatible with C.

const The **const** modifier tells the compiler that the variable that follows may not be modified.

continue The **continue** keyword is used to bypass portions of code in a loop and to force the conditional test to be performed. For example, the following **while** loop will simply read characters from the keyboard until the letter "s" is typed:

```
while(ch=getche()) {
  if(ch!='s') continue; /* read another char */
  process(ch);
}
```

The call to **process()** will not occur until **ch** contains the character "s".

default The **default** keyword is used in the **switch** statement to signal a default block of code to be executed if no matches are found in the **switch** (see the discussion of the **switch** statement).

do The **do** loop is one of three loop constructs available in C. The general form of the **do** loop is

```
do {
  statements block
} while(condition);
```

If only one statement is repeated, the braces are not necessary, but they do add clarity to the statement.

The **do** loop is the only loop in C that will always have at least one iteration, because the condition is tested at the bottom of the loop.

The **do** loop is commonly used for reading disk files. The fragment shown here will read a file until an EOF is encountered:

```
do {
  ch = getc(fp);
  store(ch);
} while(!feof(fp));
```

double The data type specifier **double** is used to declare double-precision floating point variables.

else See the discussion of the **if** statement.

enum The **enum** type specifier is used to create enumeration types. An enumeration is simply a list of objects; therefore, an enumeration type specifies what that list of objects is. An enumeration type variable may only be assigned values that are part of the enumeration list. For example, the following code declares an enumeration called **color** and a variable of that type called **c** and performs an assignment and a condition test:

```
enum color {red, green, yellow};
enum color c;

main()
{
  c = red;
  if(c==red) printf("is red\n");
}
```

extern The data type modifier **extern** is used to tell the compiler that a variable is declared elsewhere in the program. It is often used with separately compiled files that share the same global data and are linked together. In essence, **extern** notifies the compiler of a variable without redeclaring it.

For example, if **first** were declared in another file as an integer, then in subsequent files the following declaration would be used:

```
extern int first;
```

far The **far** type modifier is not part of the ANSI standard. It is used to override the default memory mode and causes its object to be compiled for a large data or code model.

float The **float** data type specifier is used to declare floating point variables.

for The **for** loop allows automatic initialization and incrementation of a counter variable. The general form is

```
for(initialization; condition; increment) {
  statement block
}
```

If the *statement block* is only one statement, the braces are not necessary.

Although **for** allows a number of variables, generally the *initialization* is used to set a counter variable to its starting value. The *condition* is generally a relational statement that checks the counter variable against a termination value, and *increment* increments (or decrements) the counter value.

The following will print the message **hello** ten times:

```
for(t=0; t<10; t++) printf("hello\n");
```

goto The **goto** keyword causes program execution to jump to the label specified in the **goto** statement. The general form of the **goto** statement is

```
goto label;
.
.
.
label:
```

All labels must end in a colon and must not conflict with keywords or function names. Furthermore, a **goto** statement can only branch within the current function, not from one function to another.

The following example will print the message **right** but not the message **wrong**:

```
goto lab1;
  printf("wrong");
lab1:
  printf("right");
```

huge The **huge** type modifier is not part of the ANSI standard. It is used to override the default memory mode and causes its object to be compiled for a large model.

if The general form of the **if** statement is

```
if(condition) {
  statement block 1
}
else {
  statement block 2
}
```

If single statements are used, the braces are not needed. The **else** is optional.

The *condition* may be any expression. If that expression evaluates to any value other than 0, then *statement block 1* will be executed; otherwise, *statement block 2* will be executed if it exists.

The following fragment checks for the letter "q," which terminates the program:

```
ch = getche();
if(ch=='q') {
  printf("program terminated");
  exit(0);
}
else proceed();
```

int The type specifier **int** is used to declare integer variables.

interrupt The **interrupt** type modifier is not part of the ANSI standard. It is used to declare functions that will be used as interrupt service routines.

long The **long** keyword is a data type modifier used to declare double-length integer variables.

near The **near** type modifier is not part of the ANSI standard. It is used to override the default memory mode and compile the modified object for a small memory model.

pascal The **pascal** keyword is not defined by the ANSI standard. It is used to force Turbo C to compile a function in such a way that its parameter passing convention is compatible with Pascal rather than C.

register The **register** keyword is a declaration modifier. If possible, it forces either an integer or a character to be stored in a register of the CPU instead of being placed in memory. It can only be used on local variables.

return The **return** statement forces a return from a function and can be used to transfer a value back to the calling routine. For example, the following function returns the pro-duct of its two integer arguments:

```
mul(int a, int b)
{
  return(a*b);
}
```

Keep in mind that as soon as a **return** is encountered, the function will return, skipping any other code that may be in the function.

sizeof The **sizeof** compile-time operator returns the length of the variable it precedes. For example,

```
printf("%d", sizeof(int));
```

will print a 2 for Turbo C on PCs.

The principal use of the **sizeof** modifier is to help generate portable code when that code depends on the size of the C built-in data types.

signed The **signed** type modifier is used to specify **signed char** or **int** data types.

short The **short** data type modifier is used for integers. In Turbo C, a short integer is the same as an integer: 2 bytes.

static The data type modifier **static** is used to instruct the compiler to create permanent storage for the local variable that it precedes. This enables the specified variable to maintain its value between function calls. When **static** is used on global variables, access to them is restricted to the file in which they are declared.

struct The **struct** keyword is used to create complex or conglomerate variables, called structures, that are made up of one or more elements of the seven basic data types. The general form of a structure is

```
struct struct_name {
  type element 1;
  type element 2;
  .
  .
  .
  type element N;
} structure_variable_name;
```

The individual elements are referenced using the dot or the arrow operator.

switch The **switch** statement is C's multiple branching statement. It is used to route execution in one of several different ways. The general form of the statement is

```
switch(control var) {
  case (constant1): statement sequence 1;
    break;
  case (constant2): statement sequence 2;
    break;
  .
  .
  .
```

```
    case (constant N): statement sequence N;
      break;
    default: default statements;

}
```

Each *statement sequence* may be from one to several statements long. The **default** portion is optional.

The **switch** statement works by checking the *control_var* against the constants. If a match is found, that sequence of statements is executed. If the **break** statement is omitted, execution will continue until the end of the **switch**. You can think of each **case** as a label. Execution will continue until a **break** statement is found or the **switch** ends. If no match is found and a **default** case is existent, its statement sequence is executed. Otherwise, no action takes place.

The following example processes a menu selection:

```
ch = getche();

switch (ch) {
  case 'e': enter();
     break;
  case 'l': list();
     break;
  case 's': sort();
     break;
  case 'q': exit(0);
  default: printf("unknown command\n");
     printf("try again\n");

}
```

typedef The **typedef** keyword allows you to create a new name for an existing data type. The data type may be either one of the built-in types or a structure or union name. The general form of **typedef** is

```
typedef type_specifier new_name;
```

For example, to use the keyword **balance** in place of **float**, you would write

```
typedef float balance;
```

union The **union** keyword is used to assign two or more variables to the same memory location. The form of the definition and the way the . (dot) and -> (arrow) operators reference an element are the same as for **struct**. The general form is

```
union union_name {
  type element 1;
  type element 2;
  .
  .
  .
  type element N;
} union variable_name;
```

unsigned The data type modifier **unsigned** tells the compiler to eliminate the sign bit of an integer or a char and to use all bits for arithmetic. This doubles the size of the largest integer or char but restricts it to only positive numbers.

void The **void** type specifier is used primarily to explicitly declare functions that return no value. It is also used to create **void** pointers, which point to any type of object.

volatile The **volatile** modifier is used to tell the compiler that a variable may have its contents altered in ways not defined explicitly by the program. For example, variables that are changed by hardware, such as real-time clocks, interrupts, or other inputs, should be declared as **volatile**.

while The **while** loop has the general form

```
while(condition) {
  statement block
}
```

If a single statement is the object of **while**, then the braces may be omitted.

The **while** tests its *condition* at the top of the loop. Therefore, if the *condition* is FALSE to begin with, the loop will not execute at all. The *condition* may be any expression.

The following example of a **while** reads 100 characters from a disk file and stores them into a character array:

```
t = 0;

while(t<100) {
  s[t] = getc(fp);
  t++;
}
```

_cs, _ds, _es, and _ss These modifiers will tell Turbo C which segment register to use for evaluating a pointer. The following example instructs the compiler to use the extra segment when using **ptr**:

```
int _es *ptr;
```

THE PREPROCESSOR AND COMPILER OPTIONS

It is possible to include various instructions to the compiler in the source code for a C program. These are called *preprocessor directives,* and although not actually part of the Turbo C language, they expand the scope of the C programming environment. Turbo C's built-in macros are also discussed in this section.

The Turbo C Preprocessor

The Turbo C preprocessor contains the following directives: **#define, #error, #include, #if, #else, #elif, #endif, #ifdef, #ifndef, #undef, #line**, and **#pragma.** These directives must begin with a # sign and must be placed at the beginning of the source line.

#define The **#define** directive is used to define an identifier and a character string that will substitute for the identifier each time it is encountered in the source file. The identifier is called a *macro name,* and the replacement process is called *macro substitution.* The general form of the directive is

```
#define macro_name string
```

Notice that there is no semicolon in this statement. There may be any number of spaces between the macro name and the string, but once the string begins, it is only terminated by a newline character.

It is common practice among C programmers to use capital letters for defined identifiers. This convention helps anyone reading the program know at a glance that a macro substitution will take place. Also, it is best to put all **#define** directives at the beginning of the file or in a separate include file, rather than sprinkling them throughout the program.

The **#define** directive has another powerful feature: the macro name can have arguments. Each time the macro name is encountered, the arguments associated with it are replaced by the actual arguments found in the program. Here is an example:

```
#define MIN(a,b)  ((a)<(b)) ? (a) : (b)

main()
{
  int x, y;

  x = 10;
  y = 20;
  printf("the minimum is: %d", MIN(x, y));
}
```

When this program is compiled, the expression defined by **MIN(a,b)** will be substituted by the **printf()** statement that uses **x** and **y** as the operands. The substituted statement will look like this:

```
printf("the minimum is: %d",(x<y) ? x : y);
```

#error When the **#error** directive is encountered, Turbo C is forced to stop compilation. This directive is used primarily for debugging, and its general form is

```
#error error_message
```

The *error_message* is not between double quotes. When the compiler encounters this directive, it displays the following information and terminates compilation:

```
Fatal: filename linenum Error directive: error_message
```

#include The **#include** preprocessor directive instructs the compiler to include another source file with the one that has the **#include** directive in it. The source file to be read in must be enclosed in double quotes or angle brackets.

If explicit path names are specified as part of the filename identifier, then only those directories will be searched for the included file. Otherwise, if the filename is enclosed in quotes, first the current working directory is searched. If the file is not found, then any directories specified on the command line are searched. Finally, if the file still has not been found, the standard directories, as they are defined by the implementation, will be searched.

If no explicit path names are specified and the filename is enclosed by angle brackets, then the file is first searched for in the directories specified in the compiler command line using the **-I** option or those specified in the integrated environment using the options menu. If the file is not found, then the standard directories are searched. At no time is the current working directory searched.

#if, #else, #elif, and #endif The general idea behind **#if** and **#else** is that if the constant expression following the **#if** is true, then the code that is between it and an **#endif** will be compiled; otherwise, it will be skipped over and the **#else** block, if present, will be compiled. The **#endif** directive is used to mark the end of an **#if** block. The general form of an **#if** block is

```
#if constant_expression
  statement sequence
#else
  statement sequence
#endif
```

If *constant_expression* is true, the block of code will be compiled; otherwise, it will be skipped.

Notice that the **#else** is used to mark both the end of the **#if** block and the beginning of the **#else** block. This is necessary because there can only be one **#endif** associated with any **#if** directive.

The **#elif** directive means "else if" and is used to establish an if/else if ladder for multiple compilation options. The **#elif** is followed by a constant expression. If the expression is TRUE, then that block of code is compiled and no other **#elif** expressions are tested. Otherwise, the next in the series is checked. The general form is

```
#if expression
  statement sequence
#elif expression 1
  statement sequence
#elif expression 2
```

```
  statement sequence
  .
  .
  .
#elif expression N
  statement sequence
#endif
```

#ifdef and #ifndef Another method of conditional compilation uses the directives **#ifdef** and **#ifndef**, which mean "if defined" and "if not defined," respectively.

The general form of **#ifdef** is

```
#ifdef macro_name
  statement sequence
#endif
```

If *macro_name* has been previously defined in a **#define** statement, the statement sequence between **#ifdef** and **#endif** will be compiled.

The general form of **#ifndef** is

```
#ifndef macro_name
  statement sequence
#endif
```

If *macro_name* is currently undefined by a **#define** statement, then the block of code is compiled.

Both **#ifdef** and **#ifndef** may use an **#else** statement but not **#elif**.

#undef The **#undef** directive is used to remove a previous definition of the macro name that follows it. The general form of **#undef** is

```
#undef macro_name
```

The principle use of **#undef** is to allow macro names to be localized to only those sections of code that need them.

#line The **#line** directive is used to change the contents of **__LINE__** and **__FILE__**, which are predefined macro names in Turbo C. **__LINE__** contains the line number of the line currently being compiled, and **__FILE__** contains the name of the file being compiled. The basic form of the **#line** directive is

```
#line number "filename"
```

where *number* is any positive integer, and the optional *filename* is any valid file identifier. The *number* is the number of the current source line, and the *filename* is the name of the source file. The **#line** directive is primarily used for debugging purposes and special applications.

#pragma The **#pragma** directive is defined by the ANSI standard to be an implementation-defined directive that allows various instructions, defined by the compiler's creator, to be given to the compiler. The general form of the **#pragma** directive is

```
#pragma name
```

where *name* is the name of the **#pragma** directive you want. Turbo C defines two **#pragma** statements: **warn** and **inline**.

The **warn** directive causes Turbo C to override warning message options. It takes the form

```
#pragma warn setting
```

where *setting* is one of the various warning error options (discussed later in this reference). For most applications you will not need to use this **#pragma**.

The second **#pragma** is **inline**. It has the general form

```
#pragma inline
```

This tells Turbo C that inline assembly code is contained in the program. For the greatest efficiency, Turbo C needs to know this in advance.

Predefined Macro Names

Turbo C specifies the following built-in predefined macro names:

__LINE__	**__LARGE__**
__FILE__	**__MEDIUM__**
__DATE__	**__MSDOS__**
__TIME__	**__PASCAL__**
__STDC__	**__SMALL__**
__CDECL__	**__TINY__**
__COMPACT__	**__TURBOC__**
__HUGE__	

The **__LINE__** and **__FILE__** macros are dicussed with **#line**. The others will be examined here.

The **__DATE__** macro contains a string of the form *month/day/year*, indicating the date on which the source file was translated into object code.

The length of time since the beginning of the compilation of the source code into object code when the **__TIME__** macro is encountered is contained as a string in **__TIME__**. The form of the string is *hour:minute:second*.

The macro **__STDC__** contains the decimal constant 1, which means that the implementation is a standard-conforming one. If it is any other number, then the implementation must vary from the standard.

The **__CDECL__** macro is defined if the standard C calling convention is used; that is, if the Pascal option is not in use. If this is not the case, then the macro is undefined.

Only one of these macros is defined, based on the memory model used during compilation: **__TINY__**, **__SMALL__**, **__COMPACT__**, **__MEDIUM__**, **__LARGE__**, and **__HUGE__**.

The **__MSDOS__** macro is defined with the value 1 under all situations when the MSDOS version of Turbo C is used.

The **__PASCAL__** macro is defined only if the Pascal calling conventions are used to compile a program. Otherwise, it is undefined.

Finally, **__TURBOC__** contains the version number of Turbo C, represented as a hexadecimal constant. The two rightmost digits represent the minor revision numbers, and the leftmost digit represents the major revision. For example, the number 202 represents version 2.02.

INTEGRATED DEVELOPMENT ENVIRONMENT (IDE)

The Integrated Development Environment, or IDE for short, provides the Turbo C user the ability to edit, compile, link, and run a program without ever leaving the Turbo C environment. The advantage to this is that extremely fast recompilation cycles can be achieved, making the creation, testing, and debugging of software easier and quicker.

Executing Turbo C

To execute the integrated version of Turbo C, simply type **TC** and then press ENTER at the DOS prompt. (After typing **TC**, you can also enter the name of the C source you wish to use.) You will then see the main menu screen, which consists of four parts from top to bottom:

- The main menu
- The editor status line and Edit window
- The compiler Message window
- The hot key quick reference line

To exit Turbo C, press ALT-X.

The rest of this section examines each part of the main menu screen.

The Main Menu

The main menu is used to instruct Turbo C to do something, such as execute the editor or compile a program, or it is used to set an environmental option. There are two ways to make a main menu selection. First, you can use the arrow keys to highlight the item you want and then press ENTER. Second, you can simply type the first letter of the menu item you want. For example, to select **Edit** you would type **E**. You may enter the letters in either upper- or lowercase. The following table summarizes what each menu selection does:

Item	Option
File	Loads and saves files, handles directories, invokes DOS, and exits Turbo C
Edit	Invokes the Turbo C editor
Run	Compiles, links, and runs the program currently loaded in the environment
Compile	Compiles the program currently in the environment
Project	Manages multifile projects
Options	Sets various compiler and linker options
Debug	Sets various debug options

To make a selection from a pull-down menu, either move the highlight to the option you desire by using the arrow keys and press ENTER, or type the capitalized letter of the selection. (This is generally, but not always, the first letter of the selection.) To exit a pull-down menu, press ESC.

Each of the main options and their suboptions is examined next.

File The **File** option has the following nine suboptions:

Load	**Save**	**Change dir**
Pick	**Write to**	**OS shell**
New	**Directory**	**Quit**

The **Load** option prompts you for a filename and then loads that file into the editor. **Pick** displays a menu that contains a list of the last eight files that you loaded into the IDE. You then use the arrow keys to highlight the file you wish to load and press ENTER to load the file.

New lets you edit a new file and erases the current contents of the editor. If the previous file has been changed but not yet saved to disk, the **New** option first asks you if you want it to save the file before erasing it. The **Save** option saves the file currently in the editor.

The **Write to** option lets you save a file by using a different filename than the one you started with. This is especially useful when you use the **New** command to begin editing a new file. The **New** command gives the file name the NONAME.C, and with the **Write to** command, you can establish the proper name for the file.

The **Directory** option displays the contents of the current working directory. You may specify a mask or use the default *.* mask. The **Change dir** command displays the path name of the current working directory and allows you to change it to another if you desire. The **OS shell** option loads the DOS command processor and lets you execute DOS commands. You must type **EXIT** to return to Turbo C. Finally, the **Quit** option quits Turbo C. (Remember, you can also use the ALT-X key combination to exit Turbo C.)

Edit Selecting the **Edit** option activates Turbo C's built-in editor. The operation of the editor is the subject of a separate section in this reference.

Run The **Run** option attempts to compile, link, and execute the program that is currently in the editor. If you have specified a project file, then **Run** invokes the Project-Make process to re-create the program. There are no other options associated with **Run**.

Compile The following five options are in the **Compile** main menu:

Compile to OBJ **Build all**
Make EXE file **Primary C file:**
Link EXE file

The **Compile to OBJ** option allows you to compile the file currently in the editor (or an alternate primary file) to an .OBJ file. (An .OBJ file is a relocatable object file that is ready to be linked into an .EXE file that can be executed.) The **Make EXE file** option will compile your program directly into an executable file. The **Link EXE file** option links the current .OBJ and library files together. The **Build all** option causes all files in a project to be recompiled and linked, whether they are out of date or not. The **Primary C file:** option lets you specify that a primary file be compiled instead of the one that happens to be loaded in the editor.

Project The **Project** option is used to aid in the development and maintenance of large, multifile programs. There are three options the **Project** main menu:

Project name
Break make on
Clear project

The **Project name** option allows you to specify the name of a project file, which contains the names of the files that comprise the project. These files will then be compiled (if necessary) and linked together to form the final executable program. For example, if a project file contains the filenames FILE1.C, FILE2.C, and FILE3.C, then all three files will be compiled and linked together to form the program. A project file is essentially the IDE version of a MAKE file used by the stand-alone MAKE utility. All project files must have the extension .PRJ.

The **Break make on** option lets you specify what type of conditions cause a project-make to stop. You can specify this option to stop the make on warnings, errors, fatal errors, or before linking.

The **Clear project** option removes the project filename from the system and resets the Message window.

Options The **Options** selection determines the way the integrated development environment operates. There are seven options in the **Options** menu:

Compiler	**Args**
Linker	**Retrieve options**
Environment	**Store options**
Directories	

Each of these entries causes another pull-down window to be displayed that contains a list of options that relate to each of these areas.

Debug The **Debug** option lets you set the way Turbo C displays compiler and linker error messages. Also, the amount of memory available for compilation is shown. You may choose the following selections from this menu:

Track messages
Clear messages
Keep messages

When working in the IDE, if a syntax error is found in your program, Turbo C prints the appropriate error message in the Message window and then highlights the line of source code that contains the error. In the Turbo C user manuals, this process is referred to as *error tracking*. By default, only the current file is tracked in this way, even if errors are found in another file, such as an include file. You can track all errors by switching the **Track messages** option to **All**, and you can turn off error tracking by switching it to **Off**.

The **Clear messages** option clears the Message window. Turning on the **Keep messages** option (which is off by default) causes Turbo C to save all error messages, appending new ones to the end. Normally, error messages are removed before each new compile.

The Edit and Message Windows

Immediately below the main menu are the Edit and Message windows. The Edit window is used by Turbo C's text editor. The Message window is beneath the Edit window and is used to display various compiler or linker messages.

The Hot Keys

At the bottom of the screen are shown the active *hot keys*—keys that are ready for use whenever you need them. The F10 key always returns you to the main menu. The other keys are discussed here.

Help The online help system is activated by pressing F1. It is context sensitive, which means that Turbo C will display information that is related to what you are currently doing. You may also select a help topic manually by pressing F1 a second time. You will be shown a list of topics from which to choose. To exit the help system, press the ESC key.

Zoom and Switching Windows By pressing the F5 key, you can enlarge either the Edit or Message window to encompass the full size of the screen. This feature simulates the zoom lens of a camera (hence its name). The F5 key is a toggle, so pressing it again returns the Edit and Message windows to their regular size.

The window that is enlarged is determined by using the F6 key, which is a toggle that switches between the Edit and Message windows. Pressing it once causes the Message window to be selected; pressing it a second time returns control to the Edit window. You will want to select the Message window to examine the various messages generated by the compiler.

Make The Make key, F9, provides a simple way to compile programs that consist of multiple source files. It will compile and/or link only the necessary modules to create an executable program. This will work reliably if you are careful to set the system time and date before you use Turbo C.

The ALT-X Key Combination You can exit Turbo C at any time by pressing the ALT-X combination.

THE TURBO C EDITOR

This section covers the text editor supplied with Turbo C's integrated programming environment. Its operation is similar to Micropro's WordStar program, as well as the editors provided by Turbo Pascal, Turbo Prolog, and SideKick. The Turbo C editor contains approximately 50 commands and is quite powerful.

Editor Commands

With few exceptions, all editor commands begin with a control character; many are then followed by another character.

For example, the sequence CTRL-Q-F is the command that tells the editor to find a string.

Invoking the Editor and Entering Text

When Turbo C begins, it waits at the sign-on message until you strike a key, and then the main menu **File** option is highlighted. To invoke the editor you either use the cursor keys to highlight **Edit**, or you simply type **e**. Press F10 to leave the editor.

When you invoke the editor, the top line is highlighted. This is the *editor status line,* and it tells you various things about the state of the editor and the file you are editing. The first two items, **Line** and **Col**, display the line number and column of the cursor. The **Insert** message is displayed when the editor is in insert mode; that is, as you enter text it will be inserted in the middle of what (if anything) is already there.

The opposite process is called *overwrite,* and in this mode of operation new text can overwrite existing text. You can toggle between these two modes by pressing the INS key. The **Indent** message indicates that autoindentation is on. (You will see how autoindentation works in a subsequent section.) You toggle the indentation mode by using the sequence CTRL-O-I. The **Tab** message means that you may insert tabs using the TAB key. This is toggled by using the sequence CTRL-O-T. The last message displays the name of the file you are editing. Once the editor has been activated, you may enter text.

Deleting Characters, Words, and Lines

You can delete a single character in two ways: with the BACKSPACE key or with the DEL key. The BACKSPACE key deletes the character immediately to the left of the cursor, while the DEL key deletes the character the cursor is under.

You can delete an entire word that is to the right of the cursor by pressing CTRL-T. A word is any set of characters delimited by one of the following characters:

space $ / - + * ' ^ [ ] ( ) . ; , < >

You can delete an entire line by pressing CTRL-Y. It does not matter where the cursor is positioned in the line—the entire line is deleted.

If you wish to delete from the current cursor position to the end of the line, press CTRL-Q-Y.

Moving, Copying, and Deleting Blocks of Text

The Turbo C editor allows you to manipulate a block of text by moving or copying it to another location or by deleting it altogether. To do any of these things, you must first define a block by moving the cursor to the start of the block and pressing CTRL-K-B. Next, move the cursor to the end of the block and press CTRL-K-K. The block that you have defined will be highlighted, or it will be in a different color if you have a color system.

To move a block of text, you place the cursor where you want the text to go and press CTRL-K-V. This causes the previously defined block of text to be deleted from its current position and placed at the new location. To copy a block, press CTRL-K-C. To delete a block that is currently marked, press CTRL-K-Y.

You may mark a single word as a block by positioning the cursor under the first character in the word and then pressing CTRL-K-T.

Cursor Movement

The Turbo C editor has a number of special cursor commands, which are summarized here:

Command	Action
CTRL-A	Moves to the start of the word that is to the left of the cursor
CTRL-S	Moves left one character
CTRL-D	Moves right one character
CTRL-F	Moves to the start of the word that is to the right of the cursor
CTRL-E	Moves the cursor up one line
CTRL-R	Moves the cursor up one full screen
CTRL-X	Moves the cursor down one line
CTRL-C	Moves the cursor down one full screen
CTRL-W	Scrolls down the screen
CTRL-Z	Scrolls up the screen
PGUP	Moves the cursor up one full screen
PGDN	Moves the cursor down one full screen
HOME	Moves the cursor to the start of the line
END	Moves the cursor to the end of the line
CTRL-Q-E	Moves the cursor to the top of the screen
CTRL-Q-X	Moves the cursor to the bottom of the screen
CTRL-Q-R	Moves the cursor to the top of the file
CTRL-Q-C	Moves the cursor to the bottom of the file

Find, and Find with Replace

To find a specific sequence of characters, press CTRL-Q-F. You will then be prompted at the status line for the string of characters you wish to find. Enter the string you are looking for, and then press ENTER. Once again, you will be prompted for search options, which modify the way the search is conducted. For example, **G2** will cause the second occurrence of the string to be found. The options are listed in the following table:

Option	Effect
B	Searches the file backwards, starting from the current cursor position
G	Searches the entire file, regardless of where the cursor is located
N	Replaces without asking; for find and replace mode only
U	Matches either upper- or lowercase
W	Matches only whole words, not substrings within words
n	Where *n* is an integer, causes the *n*th occurrence of the string to be found

No options need be specified; you may simply press ENTER. If no options are present, then the search proceeds from the current cursor position forward, with case sensitivity and substring matches allowed.

You can repeat a search by pressing CTRL-L. This is very convenient when you are looking for something specific in the file.

To activate the Find and Replace command, press CTRL-Q-A. Its operation is identical to the Find command, except it allows you to replace the string you are looking for with another. You will be prompted for a decision each time a match occurs. If you specify the **N** option, you will not be asked whether to replace each occurrence of the search string with the replacement string.

You may enter control characters into the search string by pressing CTRL-P followed by the control character.

Setting and Finding Place Markers

You can set up to four place markers in your file by pressing CTRL-K followed *by* n, where *n* is the number of the place marker (0 to 3). After a marker has been set, the command CTRL-Q followed by *n,* where *n* is the marker number, causes the cursor to go to that marker.

Saving and Loading Your File

There are three ways to save your file. First, you can exit the editor by pressing F10 and then select the **File** main menu option. In the **File** submenu, choosing the **Save** option saves what is currently in the editor into a disk file by the name shown on the status line.

Second, if you press F2 while you are using the editor, the file will be saved with the current name, and you do not need to exit the editor.

Finally, if you want to use a different filename, select the **Write to** option. This allows you to enter the name of the file to which you wish to write the current contents of the editor. It also makes this the default filename.

To load a file you may either press F3 while inside the editor or select the **Load** option in the **File** menu. Once you have done that, you will be prompted for the name of the file you wish to load. There are two ways that you can specify the filename: if you know the name, you can type it in; if you are unsure of the name, Turbo C will automatically display all files with the .C extension, and you can choose a name. Use the arrow keys to highlight the file you want, and then press ENTER.

Autoindentation

After you press ENTER the Turbo C editor will automatically place the cursor at the same indentation level as the line that was previously typed, assuming that autoindentation is on. (Remember, you toggle this feature by pressing CTRL-O-I.)

Moving Blocks of Text to and from Disk Files

To move a block of text into a disk file for later use, first define a block and then press CTRL-K-W. You will then be prompted for the name of the file in which you wish to save the block. The original block of text is not removed from your program.

To read in a block, press CTRL-K-R and enter the filename at the prompt. The contents of that file will be read in at the current cursor location.

These two commands are most useful when you are moving text between two or more files, as is so often the case during program development.

Pair Matching

Several delimiters in C work in pairs, such as { }, [ ], and ( ). In very long or complex programs, it is sometimes difficult to find the proper companion to a delimiter. In Turbo C version

1.5 or later, it is possible to have the editor find the corresponding companion delimiter automatically.

The Turbo C editor will find the companion delimiter for the following delimiter pairs: { }, [ ], ( ), < >, /* */, " ", ' '

To find the matching delimiter, place the cursor on the delimiter you wish to match, press CTRL-Q, and then type [for a forward match or] for a backward match. The editor will move the cursor to the matching delimiter.

Some delimiters can be nested, and some cannot. Those that can are { }, [ ], ( ), < >, and sometimes the comment symbols (when the nested comments option is enabled). The editor will find the proper matching delimiter in accordance with C syntax. If for some reason the editor cannot find a proper match, the cursor will not be moved.

Miscellaneous Commands

You can abort any command that requests input by pressing CTRL- U at the prompt. For example, if you execute the Find command and then change your mind, simply press CTRL-U.

If you wish to enter a control character into the file, first press CTRL-P and then the control character you want. Control characters are displayed in either low intensity or reverse video, depending on how your system is configured.

To undo changes made to a line before you have moved the cursor off that line, press CTRL-Q-L. Remember, once the cursor has been moved off the line, all changes are final.

If you wish to go to the start of a block, press CTRL-Q-B. Pressing CTRL-Q-K takes you to the end of a block.

Pressing CTRL-Q-P puts the cursor back to its previous position. This command is handy if you want to search for something and then return to where you were.

Command Summary

The following is a summary of Turbo C editor commands by category:

Command	Action
	Cursor Commands
Left arrow or CTRL-S	Left one character
Right arrow or CTRL-D	Right one character
CTRL-A	Left one word
CTRL-F	Right one word
Up arrow or CTRL-E	Up one line
Down arrow or CTRL-X	Down one line
CTRL-W	Scroll up
CTRL-Z	Scroll down
PGUP or CTRL-R	Up one page
PGDN or CTRL-C	Down one page
HOME or CTRL-Q-S	Go to start of line
END or CTRL-Q-D	Go to end of line
CTRL-Q-E	Go to top of screen
CTRL-Q-X	To go bottom of screen
CTRL-Q-R	Go to top of file
CTRL-Q-C	Go to bottom of file
CTRL Q-B	Go to start of block
CTRL-Q-K	Go to end of block
CTRL-Q-P	To go last cursor position

Command	Action
Insert Commands	
INS or CTRL-V	Toggle insert mode
ENTER or CTRL-N	Insert a blank line
Delete Commands	
CTRL-Y	Delete entire line
CTRL-Q-Y	Delete to end of line
BACKSPACE	Delete character to left
DEL or CTRL-G	Delete character at cursor
CTRL-T	Delete word to the right
Block Commands	
CTRL-K-B	Mark beginning
CTRL-K-K	Mark end
CTRL-K-T	Mark a word
CTRL-K-C	Copy a block
CTRL-K-Y	Delete a block
CTRL-K-H	Hide or display a block
CTRL-K-V	Move a block
CTRL-K-R	Write a block to disk
CTRL-K-W	Read a block from disk
CTRL-K-*N*	Set place marker, where *N* is a number 0-3
CTRL-K-P	Print block to printer

Command	Action
Find Commands	
CTRL-Q-F	Find
CTRL-A-Q	Find and replace
CTRL-Q-*N*	Find place marker, where *N* is a number 0-3
CTRL-L	Repeat find
Pair Matching	
CTRL-Q-[	Match pair forward
CTRL-Q-]	Match pair reverse
Miscellaneous Commands	
CTRL-U	Abort
CTRL-O-I	Toggle autoindentation mode
CTRL-P	Control character prefix
F10	Exit editor
F3	New file
F2	Save
CTRL-O-T	Toggle tab mode
CTRL-Q-L	Undo

IDE OPTIONS

These are the options available in the **Options** menu:

Compiler	**Args**
Linker	**Retrieve options**
Environment	**Store options**
Directories	

Each option will be examined here.

Compiler Options

After selecting **Compiler** from the **options** menu, you will see these compiler options:

Model	**Source**
Defines	**Errors**
Code generation	**Names**
Optimization	

Model The **Model** option allows you to select which memory model will be used to compile your program. The default model is the small model, which is adequate for most applications.

Defines The **Defines** option allows you to define temporary preprocessor symbols that will be used automatically by your program. You can define one or more macros by separating them with semicolons.

Code Generation Selecting the **Code generation** option presents you with a large number of switches that you can set. These are the options:

Calling convention	**Generate underbars**
Instruction set	**Merge duplicate strings**
Floating point	**Standard stack frame**
Default char type	**Test stack overflows**
Alignment	**Line numbers**

A *calling convention* is simply the method by which functions are called and arguments are passed. You can choose between C and Pascal calling conventions; generally, the C calling conventions are used.

If you know that the object code of your program will be used on an 80186 or 80286 processor, you can use the **Instruction set** option to tell Turbo C to use the 80186/80286 extended instruction set. Your program will execute a little faster, but it will not be able to run on 8088- or 8086-based computers. The default instruction set is 8088/8086.

You can control the way Turbo C implements floating point operations with the **Floating point** option. The default, and most common, method is to use 8087/80287 emulation routines. The 8087 chip is the math coprocessor for the 8086 family of CPUs, while the 80287 is the math coprocessor for the 80286 CPU. When these coprocessors are in the system, they allow very rapid floating point operations. However, if you do not have a math coprocessor, or if your program will be used in a variety of computers, the 8087's operation must be emulated in software, which is much slower. By default, the emulation mode uses the math coprocessor if one is in the system or calls the emulation routines if one is not installed.

Whether the type **char** is signed or unsigned is determined by the **Default char type** option. By default, it is signed in Turbo C.

Whether data is aligned on byte or word boundaries is determined by the **Alignment** option. On the 8086 and 80286 processors, memory accesses are quicker if data is word aligned. However, there is no difference on the 8088. The default is byte alignment.

The **Generate underbars** option, which is on by default, determines whether an underscore will be added to the start of each identifier in the link file.

A common compiler optimization that you can instruct Turbo C to perform is the elimination of duplicate string constants. That is, all identical strings can be merged into one string, resulting in smaller programs. You can control this by toggling the **Merge duplicate strings** option, which is off by default.

The **Standard stack frame** option forces Turbo C to generate standard calling and returning code for each function call to help in debugging.

You can force Turbo C to check for stack overflows by turning on the **Test stack overflow** option. This will cause your program to run slower, which may be necessary to find certain bugs. If your program crashes inexplicably from time to time, you might want to compile it with this test turned on to see if stack overflows are the problem.

Finally, you can force Turbo C to enter the number of each line of the source file into the object file. This is useful when you are using a debugger.

Optimization The **Optimization** option offers the following four toggles:

Optimize for
Use register variables
Register optimization
Jump optimization

Turbo C is very efficient, but some optimizations that make the object code smaller also make it slower. Other optimizations make the object code faster but larger. Therefore, Turbo C lets you decide which is the most important consideration by toggling the **Optimize for** option. The default is size.

When the **Use register variables** option is on, Turbo C automatically uses registers to hold variables where applicable, whether or not you have requested this explicitly by using the **register** type modifier. This option is on by default; when it is turned off, no register variables are used, even when you explicitly request it.

When the **Register optimization** option is turned on (it is off by default), Turbo C can perform some additional optimizations that prevent redundant loading and storage operations. However, Turbo C cannot know if a variable has been modified through a pointer, so you must use this option with care.

By toggling **Jump optimization** on, you allow Turbo C to rearrange the code within loops and **switch** statements. This can cause higher performance. If you are using a debugger on your object code, however, then turn this option off.

Source The **Source** option lets you set the number of significant characters in an identifier, force Turbo C to accept only the ANSI keywords, and determine if comments may be nested.

By default, Turbo C identifiers have 32 significant characters; however, you may set this number to be anywhere within the range from 1 through 32.

As you know, Turbo C supports the ANSI standard, but it has added various enhancements to the language to better support the 8086 processor. If you want to make sure that you are writing code that uses only the ANSI keywords, then toggle the option **ANSI keywords only** on. Otherwise, leave it in its default off position.

In its standard form C (including Turbo C) does not allow one comment to be inside another. The use of the **Nested comments** option is best reserved for special exceptions encountered while debugging.

Errors The **Errors** option lets you determine how errors are reported during the compilation process. Here are the seven options in this menu:

Errors: stop after	**ANSI violations**
Warnings: stop after	**Common errors**
Display warnings	**Less common errors**
Portability warnings	

You may set how many fatal errors are reported until the compilation process stops by using the **Errors: stop after** option. The default is 25. You can set how many warning errors are reported until compilation stops by using the **Warnings: stop after** option. The default setting is 100.

Turbo C is very forgiving and tries to make sense out of your source code no matter how unusual it is, but if Turbo C has a suspicion that what you have written is incorrect, it will display a warning error. A warning error does not stop compilation; it simply informs you that Turbo C is concerned about a certain construct. It is up to you to decide if Turbo C's concern is warranted.

There are four types of warning errors that may be generated. The first are portability errors, which reflect coding methods that would make it impossible to import the program to another type of processor, compiler, or Turbo C memory model. The second type of warning errors are generated by non-ANSI code practices. The third group consists of common programming errors, and the final group consists of less common programming errors. These categories are sumarized in the following table:

Portability Errors	Default
Nonportable pointer conversion	on
Nonportable pointer assignment	on
Nonportable pointer comparison	on
Constant out of range in comparison	on
Constant is long	off
Conversion may lose significant digits	off
Mixing pointers to signed and unsigned **char**	off

ANSI Violations	Default
Identifier not part of structure	on
Zero length structure	on
Void functions may not return a value	on
Both return and return of a value used	on
Suspicious pointer conversion	on
Undefined structure identifier	on
Redefinition of an identifier is not identical	on

Common Errors	Default
Function should return a value	off
Unreachable code	on
Code has no effect	on
Possible use of an identifier before definition	on
Identifier assigned value that is never used	on
Parameter identifier is never used	on
Possibly incorrect assignment	on

Less Common Errors	Default
Superfluous & with function or array	off
Identifier declared but never used	off
Ambiguous operators need parentheses	off
Structure passed by value	off
No declaration for function	off
Call to function with no prototype	off

You can toggle whether or not warning errors are displayed by using the **Display warnings** option.

Names The **Names** option lets you change the names of the various memory segments used by your program.

Linker Options

If you select the **Linker** option, you will see the following choices:

Map file	**Warn duplicate symbols**
Initialize segments	**Stack warning**
Default libraries	**Case-sensitive link**

Each option is discussed here.

Map File By default, Turbo C's linker does not create a map file of your compiled program. A map file shows the relative positions of the variables and functions that make up your program and where they reside in memory. You may need to create a map file for debugging certain programs in complex situations. You can create three kinds of map files: one that shows only the segments; one that shows the public, or global, symbols; and one that creates a detailed, or complete, map.

Initialize Segments By default, **Initialize segments** is off. It is turned on in highly specialized situations to force the linker to initialize segments.

Default Libraries The **Default libraries** option applies only when you are linking modules compiled by other C compilers. By default it is off. If you turn it on, the linker will search the libraries defined in the separately compiled modules before searching Turbo C's libraries.

Warn Duplicate Symbols By default, **Warn duplicate symbols** is on, and the linker will warn you if you have multiple-definition global identifiers. When you turn this option off, you will not see this message, and the linker will choose which definition to use.

Stack Warning If you are using Turbo C to create routines that will link with external assembly language programs or you are using the tiny memory model, you might receive the link-time message **No stack specified**. You can eliminate this message by turning **Stack warning** off.

Case-sensitive link The **Case-sensitive link** option is on by default, because C is case sensitive. If you are trying to link Turbo C modules with FORTRAN modules, however, you may need to turn this off.

Environment Options

By selecting the **Environment** option from the **Options** menu, you can change the way Turbo C's integrated environment works. The following selections are available:

Backup source files	**Zoomed windows**
Edit auto save	**Tab size**
Config auto save	**Screen Size**

When you save a file, Turbo C automatically renames the previous version of that file from a .C extension to a .BAK extension. In this way, you always have the previous version as a backup. You can turn off this option by toggling **Backup source files**. One of the few reasons you would want to turn this off is if disk space is very limited.

When **Edit auto save** is on, the editor will automatically save your source file to disk each time you run the program or use the OS Shell command. If it is off, your file will be saved only when you specifically request it. It is off by default.

When **Config auto save** is on, any changes made to the configuration file are automatically saved each time you run a program, use the OS Shell command, or exit Turbo C. If it is off, the configuration will be saved only on your command. This option is off by default.

If **Zoomed windows** is on, the Edit window will occupy the entire screen. The **Zoomed windows** option is off by default.

The default tab size is 8; you can change it by using the **Tab size** option.

Finally, if you have an EGA video adapter, you can tell Turbo C to use a 43-line display. If you have a VGA, you can use a 50-line display. The **Screen size** option is used to specify these settings, and the default is a 25-line display.

The Directories Option After selecting the **Directories** option, you will be presented with a menu consisting of these five entries:

Include directories
Library directories
Output directory
Turbo C directory
Pick file name

This option also reports the current pick file.

If you select the **Include directories** option, you may specify a list of directories that will be searched for your include files. The list may be up to 127 characters long, and each filename must be separated by a semicolon.

If you select the **Library directories** option, you may specify a list of directories that will be searched for your library files. This list may also be up to 127 characters long, and each filename must be separated by a semicolon.

Selecting the **Output directory** option allows you to specify the directory that will be used for output. The filename and path name cannot be longer than 63 characters.

You can specify where Turbo C looks for its help files and the TCCONFIG.TC file by using the **Turbo C directory** option. This filename and path name cannot be longer than 63 characters.

You can specify the path for pick files by using the **Pick file name** option.

Args

Using the **Args** option, you can run programs that use the command line arguments in the IDE. When you select **Args** you will be prompted to enter the command line parameters required by your program. After you enter the desired parameters, those command line parameters will be used each time you run the program.

COMMAND LINE VERSION

The command line version of Turbo C is called TCC.EXE. The general form of the command line is

```
TCC [option1 option2 ... optionN] fname1 fname2 ...
     fnameN
```

where *option* refers to a compiler or linker option and *fname* is either a C source file, an .OBJ file, or a library. Additional .OBJ or .LIB files on the command line are passed along to the linker for inclusion in the final program. Remember, however, that Turbo C will automatically include its standard libraries, so they need not be specified.

All compiler/linker options begin with a dash or minus sign. Generally, following an option with a dash turns that option off. The following table shows the options available in the command line version of Turbo C. Keep in mind that the options are case sensitive.

Option	Meaning
-A	Recognize ANSI keywords only
-a	Use word alignment for data
-a-	Use byte alignment for data
-B	Inline assembly code in source file
-C	Accept nested comments
-c	Compile to .OBJ only
-Dname	Define a macro name

Option	Meaning
-Dname=string	Define and give a value to a macro name
-d	Merge duplicate strings
-efname	Specify executable file name
-f	Use floating point emulation
-f-	No floating point
-f87	Use 8087
-G	Optimize code for speed
-g*n*	Stop after *n* warning errors
-Ipath	Specify the path to the include directory
-i*n*	Specify identifier length
-j*n*	Stop after *n* fatal errors
-K	**char** unsigned
-K-	**char** signed
-Lpath	Specify library directory
-M	Create map file
-mc	Use compact memory model
-mh	Use huge memory model
-ml	Use large memory model
-mm	Use medium memory model
-ms	Use small memory model
-mt	Use tiny memory model
-N	Check for stack overflows
-npath	Specify output directory
-O	Optimize for size
-p	Use Pascal calling conventions
-p-	Use C calling conventions
-r	Use register variables
-S	Generate assembly code output

Option	Meaning
-Uname	Undefine a macro name
-w	Display warning errors (see *Turbo C Reference Guide*)
-w-	Do not display warning errors
-k	Use standard stack frame
-y	Imbed line numbers into object code
-Z	Register optimization on
-z	Specify segment names (see *Turbo C Reference Guide*)
-1	Generate 80186/80286 instructions
-1-	Do not generate 80186/80286 instructions

The **-w** option allows you to set which types of warning messages will be displayed by the command line version of the compiler. By default, the command line compiler displays the same messages as the integrated version. The exact form of the **-w** command is shown in the following table:

Portability Errors	Command Line Option
Nonportable pointer assignment	**-wapt**
Nonportable pointer comparison	**-wcpt**
Constant out of range in comparison	**-wdgn**
Constant is long	**-wcln**
Conversion may lose significant digits	**-wsig**
Nonportable return type conversion	**-wrpt**

Portability Errors	**Command Line Option**
Mixing pointers to signed and unsigned **char**	**-wucp**

ANSI Violations	**Command Line Option**
Identifier not part of structure	**-wstr**
Zero length structure	**-wxst**

ANSI Violations	**Command Line Option**
Void functions may not return a value	**-wvoi**
Both return and return of a value used	**-wret**
Suspecious pointer conversion	**-wsus**
Undefined structure identifier	**-wstu**
Redefinition of an identifier is not identical	**-wdup**

Common Errors	**Command Line Option**
Function should return a value	**-wrvl**
Unreachable code	**-wrch**
Code has no effect	**-weff**
Possible use of an identifier before definition	**-wdef**
Identifier assigned a value that is never used	**-waus**

Common Errors *(continued)*	**Command Line Option**
Parameter identifier is never used	**-wpar**
Possibly incorrect assignment	**-wpia**

Less Common Errors	**Command Line Option**
Superfluous & with function or array	**-wamp**
Identifer declared but never used	**-wuse**
Ambiguous operators need parentheses	**-wamb**
Structure passed by value	**-wstv**
No declaration for function	**-wnod**
Call to function with no prototype	**-wpro**

You may specify additional object files to be linked with the source file you are compiling by specifying them after the source file. All included files must have been previously compiled and have an .OBJ extension. If you have additional libraries other than those supplied with Turbo C, you can specify them by using the .LIB extension.

TLINK: THE STAND-ALONE LINKER

Unlike the integrated development environment that has a built-in linker, the command line version of Turbo C uses a stand-alone linker called TLINK. You may not be aware of TLINK because it is loaded by the command line compiler automatically upon conclusion of a successful compilation. However, it is possible to use TLINK by itself.

TLINK is run completely from the command line and takes this general form:

```
TLINK OBJ files, output filename, map filename, libraries
```

In the first field you list all the .OBJ files you want to link together, using spaces to separate filenames on the list. The second field specifies the name of the .EXE file that will hold the output; if it is not specified, the name of the first .OBJ file is used. The *map filename* field holds the map file, which has the extension .MAP. If the map filename is not specified, the name of the .EXE file is used. Finally, the *libraries* field holds a space-separated list of libraries.

The following example links the files MYFILE1.OBJ and MYFILE2.OBJ together, using TEST.EXE as the output file and MYMAP as the map filename. No libraries are used.

```
TLINK MYFILE1 MYFILE2, TEST, MYMAP,
```

Notice that you need not use explicitly the .EXE or .MAP extension for the output or map file. The TLINK linker supplies these for you.

Although the output filename and the map filename are optional, you still must be sure to include the proper number of commas; otherwise, TLINK will not know which field is which.

Linking Turbo C Programs

Some special instructions apply to TLINK when you want to use it manually to link object files produced by Turbo C into an executable program. First, every time a Turbo C program is linked, the first object file on the link line must be one of

Turbo C's initialization modules. For each memory model supported by Turbo C, there is a module that must agree with the type of memory model used to compile the program. The modules' names and their associated memory models are shown here:

Initialization Module Name	Memory Model
C0T.OBJ	Tiny
C0S.OBJ	Small
C0C.OBJ	Compact
C0M.OBJ	Medium
C0L.OBJ	Large
C0H.OBJ	Huge

The second thing you need to ensure is that the proper standard library file is linked. Like the initialization module, it too must agree with the memory model used to compile the program. The library files are shown here:

Library Name	Memory Model
CS.LIB	Tiny
CS.LIB	Small
CC.LIB	Compact
CM.LIB	Medium
CL.LIB	Large
CH.LIB	Huge

If your program uses any floating point numbers, you will need to include on the link line either EMU.LIB or FP87.LIB (the latter is used only for an 8087/80287).

The mathematics routines are contained in MATH*x*.LIB, where *x* is one of the following letters corresponding to the proper memory model: t, s, c, m, l, h. Remember, the memory model used to compile your program must agree with that of the library.

Given this information, a program file called TCTEST that uses floating point emulation, has no math routines, and uses the small memory model can be linked together with the following link line:

```
TLINK C0S TCTEST, , , EMU MATHS CS
```

TLINK Options TLINK supports eight options, each consisting of a slash followed by a letter. These options may be placed at any point in the TLINK command line. For example, this link line will not produce a map file but will cause source code line numbers to be included in the map file:

```
TLINK /x /l C0s MYFILE, ; , CS
```

The following table is a summary of the TLINK options:

Option	Meaning
/c	Case is significant in PUBLIC and EXTRN symbols
/d	Display warning if duplicate symbols are found in the libraries
/i	Initialize all segments
/l	Include source line numbers for debugging
/m	Include public symbols in map file
/n	Ignore the default libraries
/s	Include detailed segment map in map file
/x	Do not create a map file

I/O FUNCTIONS

The functions that constitute the Turbo C input/output system can be grouped into three major categories: console I/O, UNIX-like unbuffered file I/O, and buffered file I/O. Console I/O functions are special-case versions of the more general functions found in the buffered file system. It is sometimes easier for beginners to think of console I/O routines as separate from the file routines; however, remember that a common interface is used for the console and file I/O functions.

The unbuffered UNIX-like I/O system is not defined by the proposed ANSI standard and is expected to decline in popularity. This system's functions are included here because they are still widely used in existing programs. The UNIX-like file system and the buffered file system are completely separate. The UNIX-like file system operates via file descriptors, or handles, and its use should be clear.

The buffered file system is designed to work with a wide variety of devices, including terminals, disk drives, and tape drives. Even though each device is very different, the buffered file system transforms each into a logical device called a *stream*. All streams are similar in behavior and are largely device independent, so functions that write to a disk file can also write to the console. There are two types of streams: text and binary.

A *text stream* is a sequence of characters organized into lines that are terminated by newline characters. In a text stream, certain character translations may occur as required by the host environment. For example, a newline may be converted to a carriage-return/linefeed pair. Therefore, there may not be a one-to-one relationship between the characters that are written (or read) and those in the external device. Also, because of possible translations, the number of characters written (or read) may not be the same as those found in the external device.

A *binary stream* is a sequence of bytes that have a one-to-one correspondence to those found in the external device. That is, no character translations will occur. Also, the number of bytes written (or read) will be the same as found in the external device.

At the beginning of a program's execution, the following five predefined text streams are opened: **stdin, stdout, stdaux, stdprn,** and **stderr**. They refer to the standard I/O devices connected to the system. These streams may be redirected by the operating system, and you should never try explicitly to open or close files associated with these streams.

Each stream that is associated with a file has a file control structure of type **FILE**. This structure is defined in the header **stdio.h**. No programmer modifications to this file control block, or manipulations of it, should ever be undertaken.

#include <stdio.h>
► void clearerr(FILE *stream)

The **clearerr()** function is used to reset to zero (off) the file error flag pointed to by *stream*. The end-of-file indicator is also reset.

The error flags for each stream are initially set to zero by a successful call to **fopen()**. Once an error has occurred, the flags stay set until an explicit call to either **clearerr()** or **rewind()** is made.

File errors can occur for a wide variety of reasons, many of which are system dependent. The exact nature of the error can be determined by calling **perror()**, which displays what error has occurred.

Related functions: **feof()**, **ferror()**, **perror()**.

#include <io.h>
► int close(int fd)

The **close()** function belongs to the UNIX-like file system and is not defined by the proposed ANSI standard. When **close()** is called with a valid file descriptor, it closes the file associated with it and flushes the write buffers, if applicable. File descriptors are created through a successful call to **open()** or **creat()** and do not relate to streams or file pointers.

When successful, **close()** returns a 0; otherwise, a -1 is returned. Although there are several reasons that a file may not be able to be closed, the most common is the premature removal of the medium. For example, if a diskette is removed from the drive before the file is closed, an error will result.

Related functions: **open()**, **creat()**, **read()**, **write()**, **unlink()**.

#include <io.h>
► int creat(char *filename, int pmode)

The **creat()** function is part of the UNIX-like file system and is not defined by the proposed ANSI standard. Its purpose is to create a new file with the name pointed to by *filename* and to open it for writing. When successful **creat()** returns a file descriptor that is greater than or equal to 0; when it fails a -1 is returned. (File descriptors are integers and do not relate to streams or file pointers.)

The value of *pmode* determines the file's access setting, sometimes called its *permission mode*. The value of *pmode* must be one of these macros (defined in **stat.h**):

Value	Meaning
S_IWRITE	Write access
S_IREAD	Read access
S_IREAD | S_IWRITE	Read/write access

Related functions: **open()**, **close()**, **read()**, **write()**, **unlink()**, **eof()**.

```
#include <io.h>
int eof(int fd)
```

The **eof()** function is part of the UNIX-like file system and is not defined by the proposed ANSI standard. When called with a valid file descriptor, **eof()** returns a 1 if the end of the file has been reached; otherwise, a 0 is returned. If an error has occurred, a -1 is returned.

Related functions: **open()**, **close()**, **read()**, **write()**, **unlink()**.

```
#include <stdio.h>
int fclose(FILE *stream)
int fcloseall(void)
```

The **fclose()** function closes the file associated with *stream* and flushes its buffer. After an **fclose()**, *stream* is no longer connected with the file and any automatically allocated buffers are deallocated.

If **fclose()** is successful, a 0 is returned; otherwise, EOF is returned. Trying to close a file that has already been closed is an error.

The **fcloseall()** function closes all open files. When successful it returns the number of files closed; EOF is returned if an error occurs.

Related functions: **fopen()**, **freopen()**, **fflush()**.

#include <stdio.h>
int feof(FILE *stream)

The **feof()** function checks the file position indicator to determine if the end of the file associated with *stream* has been reached. A nonzero value is returned if the file position indicator is at end-of-file; a 0 is returned otherwise.

Once the end of the file has been reached, subsequent read operations will return EOF until either **rewind()** is called or the file position indicator is moved by means of **fseek()**.

The **feof()** function is particularly useful when you are working with binary files, because the end-of-file marker is also a valid binary integer. Explicit calls must be made to **feof()** rather than simply testing the return value of **getc()**.

Related functions: **clearerr()**, **ferror()**, **perror()**, **putc()**, **getc()**.

#include <stdio.h>
int ferror(FILE *stream)

The **ferror()** function checks for a file error on the given *stream*. A return value of 0 indicates that no error has occurred, and a nonzero value indicates an error.

The error flags associated with *stream* will stay set either until the file is closed or until **rewind()** or **clearerr()** is called.

To determine the exact nature of the error, use the **perror()** function.

Related functions: **clearerr(), feof(), perror()**.

#include <stdio.h>
int fflush(FILE *stream)

If *stream* is associated with a file opened for writing, a call to **fflush()** causes the contents of the output buffer to be physically written to the file. If *stream* points to an input file, then the contents of the input buffer are cleared. In either case the file remains open.

A return value of 0 indicates success, while EOF indicates that an error has occurred.

All buffers are automatically flushed upon normal termination of the program or when they are full. Also, closing a file flushes its buffer.

Related functions: **fclose(), fopen(), fread(), fwrite(), getc(), putc()**.

#include <stdio.h>
► int fgetc(FILE *stream)

The **fgetc()** function returns the next character from the input *stream* from the current position and increments the file position indicator. The character is read as an **unsigned char** that is converted to an integer.

If the end of the file is reached, **fgetc()** returns EOF. Since EOF is a valid integer value, however, you must use **feof()** to check for end-of-file when working with binary files. If **fgetc()** encounters an error, EOF is also returned. Again, if working with binary files, you must use **ferror()** to check for file errors.

Related functions: **fputc()**, **getc()**, **putc()**, **fopen()**.

#include <stdio.h>
► char *fgets(char *str, int num, FILE *stream)

The **fgets()** function reads up to *num*-1 characters from *stream* and places them into the character array pointed to by *str*. Characters are read until either a newline or an EOF is received or until the specified limit is reached. After the characters have been read, a null is placed in the array immediately after the last character read. A newline character will be retained and will be part of *str*.

If successful, **fgets()** returns *str*; a null pointer is returned upon failure. If a read error occurs, the contents of the array pointed to by *str* are indeterminate. Because a null pointer will be returned when either an error has occurred or when the end of the file is reached, you should use **feof()** or **ferror()** to determine what has actually happened.

Related functions: **fputs()**, **fgetc()**, **gets()**, **puts()**.

```
#include <stdio.h>
FILE *fopen(const char *fname,
        const char *mode)
```

The **fopen()** function opens a file whose name is pointed to by *fname* and returns the stream that is associated with it. The type of operations that will be allowed on the file are defined by the value of *mode*. The legal values for *mode* are shown in the following table. The filename must be a string of characters that define a valid filename and path specification.

Mode	Meaning
"r"	Open text file for reading
"w"	Create a text file for writing
"a"	Append to text file
"rb"	Open binary file for reading
"wb"	Create binary file for writing
"ab"	Append to a binary file
"r+"	Open text file for read/write
"w+"	Create text file for read/write
"a+"	Open text file for read/write
"r+b"	Open binary file for read/write
"w+b"	Create binary file for read/write
"a+b"	Open binary file for read/write

As this table shows, a file may be opened in either text or binary mode. In text mode, carriage-return/linefeed sequences are translated to newline characters on input. On output, the reverse occurs: newlines are translated to carriage-return/linefeeds. No such translations occur on binary files.

If **fopen()** is successful in opening the specified file, then a **FILE** pointer is returned. If the file cannot be opened, a null pointer is returned.

Related functions: **fclose()**, **fread()**, **fwrite()**, **putc()**, **getc()**.

#include <stdio.h>
► **int fprintf(FILE *stream, char *format, arg_list)**

The **fprintf()** function outputs the values of the arguments contained in *arg_list*, as specified in the *format* string, to the stream pointed to by *stream*. The return value is the number of characters actually printed. If an error occurs, a negative number is returned.

There may be from zero to several arguments; the maximum number is system dependent.

The operations of the format control string and commands are identical to those in **printf()**. See the **printf()** function for a complete description.

Related functions: **printf()**, **fscanf()**.

#include <stdio.h>
► **int fputc(int ch, FILE *stream)**

The **fputc()** function writes the character *ch* to the specified stream at the current file position, and then advances the file position indicator. Even though *ch* is declared to be an **int**, it is converted by **fputc()** into an **unsigned char**. (Because all character arguments are elevated to integers at the time of the call, you will generally see character variables used as arguments. If an integer were used, the high-order byte would simply be discarded.)

The value returned by **fputc()** is the value of the character written. If an error occurs, EOF is returned. For files opened for binary operations, an EOF may be a valid character, and the **ferror()** function will need to be used to determine whether an error has actually occurred.

Related functions: **fgetc()**, **fopen()**, **fprintf()**, **fread()**, **fwrite()**.

#include <stdio.h>
► int fputchar(int ch)

The **fputchar()** function writes the character *ch* to **stdout**. Even though *ch* is declared to be an **int**, it is converted by **fputchar()** into an **unsigned char**. (Because all character arguments are elevated to integers at the time of the call, you will generally see character variables used as arguments. If an integer were used, the high-order byte would simply be discarded.) A call to **fputchar()** is the functional equivalent of a call to **fputc(ch, stdout)**.

The value returned by **fputchar()** is the value of the character written. If an error occurs, EOF is returned. For files opened for binary operations, an EOF may be a valid character, and the function **ferror()** will need to be used to determine whether an error has actually occurred.

Related functions: **fgetc()**, **fopen()**, **fprintf()**, **fread()**, **fwrite()**.

#include <stdio.h>
int fputs(char *str, FILE *stream)

The **fputs()** function writes the contents of the string pointed to by *str* to the specified stream. The null terminator is not written.

The **fputs()** function returns the last character written on success and an EOF on failure.

Related functions: **fgets()**, **gets()**, **puts()**, **fprintf()**, **fscanf()**.

#include <stdio.h>
int fread(void *buf, int size, int count,
FILE *stream)

The **fread()** function reads *count* number of objects from the stream pointed to by *stream* and places them in the character array pointed to by *buf*. Each object is *size* number of characters in length. The file position indicator is advanced by the number of characters read.

The **fread()** function returns the number of items actually read. If fewer items are read than were requested in the call, either an error has occurred or the end of the file has been reached. You must use **feof()** or **ferror()** to determine what has taken place.

If the stream is opened for text operations, then carriage-return/linefeed sequences are automatically translated into newlines.

Related functions: **fwrite()**, **fopen()**, **fscanf()**, **fgetc()**, **getc()**.

#include <stdio.h>
FILE *freopen(const char *fname, const char *mode, FILE *stream)

The **freopen()** function is used to associate an existing stream with a different file. The new file's name is pointed to by *fname,* the access mode is pointed to by *mode,* and the stream to be reassigned is pointed to by *stream*. The *mode* string uses the same format as **fopen()**; a complete discussion is found in the **fopen()** description.

The **freopen()** function returns a pointer to *stream* on success and a null pointer otherwise.

The main use of **freopen()** is to redirect the system-defined files **stdin, stdout,** and **stderr** to some other file.

Related functions: **fopen(), fclose()**.

#include <stdio.h>
int fscanf(FILE *stream, const char *format, arg_list)

The **fscanf()** function works exactly like the **scanf()** function except that it reads the information from the stream specified by *stream* instead of **stdin**. See the **scanf()** function for details.

The **fscanf()** function returns the number of arguments actually assigned values. This number does not include skipped fields. A return value of EOF means that an attempt was made to read past the end of the file.

Related functions: **scanf(), fprintf()**.

```
#include <stdio.h>
int fseek(FILE *stream, long offset,
      int origin)
```

The **fseek()** function sets the file position indicator associated with *stream* according to the values of *offset* and *origin*. Its main purpose is to support random I/O operations. The *offset* is the number of bytes from *origin* to make the new position. The *origin* is either a 0, indicating the start of the file, a 1, for the current position, or a 2, indicating the end of the file. Turbo C defines the following macros for *origin*:

Macro	Origin
SEEK_SET	Beginning of file
SEEK_CUR	Current position
SEEK_END	End of file

A return value of 0 means that **fseek()** succeeded. A nonzero value indicates failure.

According to the proposed ANSI standard, **fseek()** should not be used on text files because the character translations will cause position errors to result. Therefore, its use is suggested only on binary files.

You may use **fseek()** to move the position indicator anywhere in the file, even beyond the end. It is an error, however, to set the position indicator before the beginning of the file.

The **fseek()** function clears the end-of-file flag associated with the specified stream. Furthermore, it nullifies any prior **ungetc()** on the same stream; see **ungetc()**.

Related functions: **ftell()**, **rewind()**, **fopen()**.

#include <stdio.h>
long ftell(FILE *stream)

The **ftell()** function returns the current value of the file position indicator for the specified stream. When an error occurs, the functon returns -1L.

Related functions: **fseek()**.

#include <stdio.h>
int fwrite(const void *buf, int size,
int count, FILE *stream)

The **fwrite()** function writes *count* number of objects to the stream pointed to by *stream* from the character array pointed to by *buf*. Each object is *size* number of characters in length. The file position indicator is advanced by the number of characters written.

The **fwrite()** function returns the number of items actually written, which, if the function is successful, will equal the number requested. If fewer items are written than have been requested, an error has occurred. For text streams, various character translations may take place but will have no effect on the return value.

Related functions: **fread()**, **fscanf()**, **getc()**, **fgetc()**.

#include <stdio.h>
int getc(FILE *stream)
int getch(void)
int getche(void)

The **getc()** macro returns the next character from the input *stream* from the current position and increments the file position indicator. The character is read as an **unsigned char** that is converted to an integer.

If the end of the file is reached, **getc()** returns EOF. Since EOF is a valid integer value, however, you must use **feof()** to check for end-of-file when working with binary files. If **getc()** encounters an error, EOF is also returned. When working with binary files, you must use **ferror()** to check for file errors.

The **getch()** function reads a single character from the keyboard and echoes the key. The **getche()** function reads a single character from the keyboard but does not echo the key. Both functions return the character read.

Related functions: **fputc()**, **fgetc()**, **putc()**, **fopen()**.

#include <stdio.h>
▶ int getchar(void)

The **getchar()** macro returns the next character from **stdin**. It is functionally equivalent to **getc(stdin)**. The character is read as an **unsigned char** that is converted to an integer.

If the end of the file is reached, **getc()** returns EOF. Since EOF is a valid integer value, however, you must use **feof()** to check for end-of-file when working with binary files. If **getc()** encounters an error, EOF is also returned. When working with binary files, you must use **ferror()** to check for file errors.

Related functions: **fputc()**, **fgetc()**, **putc()**, **fopen()**.

#include <stdio.h>
▶ char *gets(char *str)

The **gets()** function reads characters from **stdin** and places them into the character array pointed to by *str*. Characters are read until a newline or an EOF is received. The newline character is not made part of the string; instead, it is translated into a null to terminate the string.

If successful, **gets()** returns *str*; a null pointer is returned on failure. If a read error occurs, the contents of the array pointed to by *str* are indeterminate. Because a null pointer will be returned either when an error has occurred or when the end of the file is reached, you should use **feof()** or **ferror()** to determine what has actually happened.

There is no limit to the number of characters that **gets()** will read; it is therefore your job to make sure that the array pointed to by *str* will not be overrun.

Related functions: **fputs()**, **fgetc()**, **fgets()**, **puts()**.

#include <stdio.h>
int getw(FILE *stream)

The **getw()** function is not defined by the proposed ANSI standard, and its use may cause portability problems.

The **getw()** function returns the next integer from *stream* and advances the file position indicator appropriately.

Because the integer read may have a value equal to EOF, you must use **feof()** or **ferror()** to determine when end-of-file is reached or whether an error has occurred.

Related functions: **putw()**, **fread()**.

#include <conio.h>
int kbhit(void)

The **kbhit()** function is not defined by the proposed ANSI standard. It returns a nonzero value if a key has been pressed at the console and returns 0 otherwise. Its main use is to allow a user to interrupt a program.

Related functions: **fgetc()**, **getc()**.

#include <io.h>
► long lseek(int fd, long offset, int origin)

The **lseek()** function is part of the UNIX-like I/O system and is not defined by the proposed ANSI standard.

The **lseek()** function sets the file position indicator to the location specified by *offset* and by *origin* for the file that is specified by *fd*.

How **lseek()** works depends on the values of *origin* and *offset*. The *origin* may be either 0, 1, or 2. This table explains how *offset* is interpreted for each *origin* value:

Origin	Effect of Call to lseek()
0	Count the offset from the start of the file
1	Count the offset from the current position
2	Count the offset from the end of the file

(You may use the macros **SEEK_SET**, **SEEK_CUR**, and **SEEK_END**, defined in **io.h**, instead of the actual values for *origin*, if you prefer.)

The **lseek()** function returns *offset* on success. Therefore, **lseek()** will be returning a long integer and must be declared as such at the top of your program. Upon failure, a -1L is returned.

Related functions: **read()**, **write()**, **open()**, **close()**.

#include <io.h>
► int open(char *fname, int access, int mode)

The **open()** function is part of the UNIX-like I/O system and is not defined by the proposed ANSI standard.

Unlike the buffered I/O system, the UNIX-like system does not use file pointers of type **FILE**, but rather file descriptors of type **int**. The **open()** function opens a file with the name *fname* and sets its access mode as specified by *access*. These are the macros defined for *access,* defined in **fcntl.h**:

Access	Effect
O_RDONLY	Read
O_WRONLY	Write
O_RDWR	Read/write
O_NDELAY	Not used
O_APPEND	Write at end of file
O_CREAT	Create file
O_TRUNC	Truncate file
O_EXCL	OR with O_CREAT, error returned if file exists
O_BINARY	Binary file
O_TEXT	Text file

The *mode* is only necessary if you call **open()** with an *access* value of **O_CREAT**. The *mode* parameter may take these values (defined in **stat.h**):

Mode	Meaning
S_IWRITE	Write access
S_IREAD	Read access
S_IREAD | S_IWRITE	Read/write access

A successful call to **open()** returns a positive integer that is the file descriptor associated with the file. A return value of -1 means that the file cannot be opened.

Related functions: **close()**, **read()**, **write()**.

#include <stdio.h>
int printf(const char *format, arg_list)

The **printf()** function writes to **stdout** the arguments that comprise *arg_list* under the control of the string pointed to by *format*.

The string pointed to by *format* consists of two types of items. The first type is made up of characters that will be printed on the screen. The second type contains format commands that define the way the arguments are displayed. A format command consists of a percent sign (%) followed by the format code. The format commands are shown in the following table:

Code	Format
%c	Single character
%d	Decimal
%i	Decimal
%e	Scientific notation
%f	Decimal floating point
%g	Uses **%e** or **%f**, whichever is shorter

Code	Format
%o	Octal
%s	String of characters
%u	Unsigned decimal
%x	Hexadecimal
%%	Prints a % sign
%p	Displays a pointer
%n	The associated argument must be an integer pointer, into which the number of characters written so far is placed

There must be exactly the same number of arguments as there are format commands, and the format commands and the arguments are matched in order. For example, the **printf()** call

```
printf("Hi %c %d %s",'c',10,"there!");
```

displays **Hi c 10 there!**

If there are insufficient arguments to match the format commands, the output is undefined. If there are more arguments than format commands, the remaining arguments are discarded.

The **printf()** function returns the number of characters actually printed. A negative return value indicates that an error has taken place.

The format commands may have modifiers that specify the field width, the number of decimal places, and a left justification flag. An integer placed between the % (percent sign) and the format command acts as a *minimum field width specifier*. This pads the output with blanks or zeros to ensure that it is at least a certain minimum length. If the string or number is greater than that minimum, it will be printed in full, even if it overruns the minimum.

The default padding is done with spaces. If you wish to pad with zeros, place a zero before the field width specifier. For example, **%05d** will pad a number of less than five digits with zeros so that its total length is five.

To specify the number of decimal places printed for a floating point number, place a decimal point followed by the number of decimal places you wish to display after the field width specifier. For example, **%10.4f** will display a number at least ten characters wide with four decimal places. When this is applied to strings or integers, the number following the period specifies the maximum field length. For example, **%5.7s** will display a string that will be at least five characters long and will not exceed seven. If the string is longer than the maximum field width, the characters will be truncated at the end.

By default, all output is right justified; that is, if the field width is larger than the data printed, the data will be placed on the right edge of the field. You can force the information to be left justified by placing a minus sign directly after the %. For example, **%-10.2f** will left justify a floating point number with two decimal places in a ten-character field.

There are two format command modifiers that allow **printf()** to display short and long integers. These modifiers may be applied to the **d, i, o, u,** and **x** type specifiers. The **l** modifier tells **printf()** that a long data type follows; for example, **%ld** means that a long integer is to be displayed. The **h** modifier tells **printf()** to display a short integer. Therefore, **%hu** means that the data is of type **short unsigned int**.

The **l** modifier may also prefix the floating point commands **e, f,** and **g** and indicates that a **double** follows.

The **%n** command causes the number of characters that have been written at the time the **%n** is encountered to be placed in an integer variable whose pointer is specified in the argument list. For example, this code fragment displays the number 14 after the line **this is a test**:

```
int i;

printf("this is a test%n",&i);
printf("%d",i);
```

Related functions: **scanf()**, **fprintf()**

#include <stdio.h>
int putc(int ch, FILE *stream)

The **putc()** function writes the character contained in the least significant byte of *ch* to the output stream pointed to by *stream*. Because character arguments are elevated to integer at the time of the call, you may use character variables as arguments to **putc()**.

The **putc()** function returns the character written on success or EOF if an error occurs. If the output stream has been opened in binary mode, then EOF is a valid value for *ch*. This means that you must use **ferror()** to determine if an error has occurred.

The **putc()** function is often implemented as a macro with **fputc()** substituting it, because **fputc()** is functionally equivalent to **putc()**.

Related functions: **fgetc()**, **fputc()**, **getchar()**, **putchar()**.

#include <stdio.h>
int putchar(int ch)

The **putchar()** macro writes the character contained in the least significant byte of *ch* to **stdout.** It is functionally equivalent to **putc(ch,stdout).** Because character arguments are elevated to integer at the time of the call, you may use character variables as arguments to **putchar().**

The **putchar()** macro returns the character written on success or EOF if an error occurs. If the output stream has been opened in binary mode, then EOF is a valid value for *ch.* This means that you must use **ferror()** to determine if an error has occurred.

Related functions: **fputchar(), putc().**

#include <stdio.h>
int puts(const char *str)

The **puts()** function writes the string pointed to by *str* to the standard output device. The null terminator is translated to a newline.

The **puts()** function returns a newline if successful and an EOF upon failure.

Related functions: **putc(), gets(), printf().**

#include <stdio.h>
int putw(int i, FILE *stream)

The **putw()** function is not defined by the proposed ANSI standard and may not be fully portable. It writes the integer *i* to *stream* at the current file position and increments the file position pointer appropriately.

The **putw()** function returns the value written. A return value of EOF means an error has occurred in the stream if it is in text mode. Because EOF is also a valid integer value, you must use **ferror()** to detect an error in a binary stream.

Related functions: **getw(), printf(), fwrite()**.

#include <io.h>
int read(int fd, void *buf, int count)

The **read()** function is part of the UNIX-like I/O system and is not defined by the proposed ANSI standard. It reads *count* number of bytes from the file described by *fd* into the buffer pointed to by *buf*. The file position indicator is adjusted forward by the number of bytes read. If the file is opened in text mode, then character translations may take place.

The return value will be equal to the number of bytes actually read. This number may be smaller than *count* if either an end-of-file or an error is encountered. A value of -1 indicates an error, and a value of 0 is returned if an attempt is made to read at end-of-file.

Related functions: **open(), close(), write(), lseek()**.

#include <stdio.h>
int remove(char *fname)

The **remove()** macro erases the file specified by *fname*. It returns a 0 if the file was successfully deleted and a -1 if an error occurred.

Related functions: **rename(), unlink()**.

#include <stdio.h>
int rename(const char *oldfname, const char *newfname)

The **rename()** function changes the name of the file specified by *oldfname* to *newfname*. The *newfname* must not match any existing directory entry.

The **rename()** function returns 0 if successful and -1 if an error has occurred.

Related function: **remove()**.

#include <stdio.h>
void rewind(FILE *stream)

The **rewind()** function moves the file position indicator to the start of the specified stream. It also clears the end-of-file and error flags associated with *stream*. It returns 0 if successful; a nonzero return indicates failure.

Related function: **fseek()**.

#include <stdio.h>
int scanf(const char *format, arg_list)

The **scanf()** is a general-purpose input routine that reads the stream **stdin.** It can read all the built-in data types and automatically convert them into the proper internal format. It is much like the reverse of **printf()**.

The control string pointed to by *format* consists of three classifications of characters:

- Format specifiers
- White-space characters

- Non-white-space characters

The input format specifiers are preceded by a % sign and tell **scanf()** what type of data is to be read next. For example, **%s** reads a string, while **%d** reads an integer. These codes are listed in the following table:

Code	Meaning
%c	Read a single character
%d	Read a decimal integer
%i	Read a decimal integer
%e	Read a floating point number
%f	Read a floating point number
%h	Read a short integer
%o	Read an octal number
%s	Read a string
%x	Read a hexadecimal number
%p	Read a pointer
%n	Receive an integer value equal to the number of characters read so far

The format string is read left to right and the format codes are matched, in order, with the arguments in the argument list.

A white-space character is either a space, a tab, or a newline. One white-space character in the control string will cause **scanf()** to read, but not store, any number (including zero) of white-space characters up to the first non-white-space character.

A non-white-space character causes **scanf()** to read and discard a matching character. For example, **%d,%d** causes **scanf()** to first read an integer, then read and discard a comma, and, finally, read another integer. If the specified character is not found, **scanf()** will terminate.

All the variables used to receive values through **scanf()** must be passed by their addresses. This means that all arguments must be pointers to the variables used as arguments. This is C's way of creating a "call by reference," and it allows a function to alter the contents of an argument. For example, if you wish to read an integer into the variable **count**, you would use the following **scanf()** call:

```
scanf("%d",&count);
```

Strings will be read into character arrays, and the array name, without any index, is the address of the first element of the array. Thus, to read a string into the character array *address,* you would use

```
scanf("%s",address);
```

In this case, *address* is already a pointer and need not be preceded by the & operator.

The input data items must be separated by spaces, tabs, or newlines. Punctuation marks, such as commas or semicolons, do not count as separators. This means that

```
scanf("%d%d",&r,&c);'
```

will accept an input of **10 20** but will fail with **10,20**. As in **printf()**, the **scanf()** format codes are matched in order with the variables receiving the input in the argument list.

An * placed after the % and before the format code will read data of the specified type but suppress its assignment. For example, given the input **10/20**,

```
scanf("%d%*c%d",&x,&y);
```

will place the value 10 into **x**, discard the divide sign, and give **y** the value 20.

The format commands can specify a maximum field length modifier. This is an integer number placed between the % and the format command code that limits the number of characters read for any field. For example, if you wish to read no more than 20 characters into *address*, then you would write

```
scanf("%20s",address);
```

If the input stream was greater than 20 characters, then a subsequent call to input would begin where this call left off. For example, if

```
1100_Parkway_Ave,_apt_2110_B
```

had been entered as the response to the earlier **scanf()** call, only the first 20 characters, or up to the "p" in "apt," would have been placed into *address* because of the maximum size specifier. This means that the remaining eight characters, "t_2110_B," have not yet been used. If another **scanf()** call is made, such as

```
scanf("%s",str);
```

then "t_2110_B" would be placed into *str*. Input for a field may terminate before the maximum field length is reached if a white-space character is encountered. In this case, **scanf()** moves on to the next field.

Although spaces, tabs, and newlines are used as field separators, these are read like any other character when reading a single character. For example, with an input stream of

x y, the following will return with the character "x" in **a**, a space in **b**, and the character "y" in **c**:

```
scanf("%c%c%c", &a, &b, &c);
```

Be careful: Any other characters in the control string—including spaces, tabs, and newlines—will be used to match and discard characters from the input stream. Any character that matches is discarded. This example has the input stream **10t20** and will place 10 into **x** and 20 into **y**. The "t" is discarded because of the "t" in the control string.

```
scanf("%st%s",&x,&y);
```

Here is another example:

```
scanf("%s ",name);
```

This will not return until you type a terminator followed by a character. This is because the space after the **%s** has instructed **scanf()** to read and discard spaces, tabs, and newline characters.

The **scanf()** function returns a number equal to the number of fields that were successfully assigned values. When the * modifier is used to suppress the assignment, this number will not include fields that were read but not assigned. A return value of EOF is returned if an attempt is made to read at the end-of-file mark. A value of 0 is returned if no fields were assigned.

Related functions: **printf()**, **fscanf()**.

#include <stdio.h>
void setbuf(FILE *stream, char *buf)

The **setbuf()** function is used either to indicate the buffer the specified stream will use or, if called with *buf* set to null, to turn off buffering. If a programmer-defined buffer is to be specified, then it must be **BUFSIZ** characters long; **BUFSIZ** is defined in **stdio.h**.

The **setbuf()** function returns no value.

Related functions: **fopen()**, **fclose()**, **setvbuf()**.

#include <stdio.h>
int setvbuf(FILE *stream, char *buf,
int mode, unsigned size)

The **setvbuf()** function allows you to specify the buffer, its size, and its mode for the specified stream. The character array pointed to by *buf* is used as *stream*'s buffer for I/O operations. The size of the buffer is set by *size,* and *mode* determines how buffering will be handled. If *buf* is null, no buffering will take place.

The legal values of *mode* are **_IOFBF**, **_IONBF**, and **_IOLBF**. These are defined in **stdio.h**. When the mode is set to **_IOFBF**, then full buffering will take place. This is the default setting. When set to **_IONBF**, the stream will be unbuffered, regardless of the value *buf*. If *mode* is **_IOLBF**, then the stream will be line-buffered, which means that the buffer will be flushed each time a newline character is written for output streams. For input streams, an input request reads all characters up to a newline. In either case, the buffer is also flushed when full.

The value of *size* must be greater than 0.

The **setvbuf()** function returns 0 on success and a nonzero value on failure.

Related function: **setbuf()**.

#include <stdio.h>
int sprintf(char *buf, const char *format, arg_list)

The **sprintf()** function is identical to **printf()** except that the generated output is placed into the array pointed to by *buf*. See the **printf()** function.

The return value is equal to the number of characters actually placed into the array.

Related functions: **printf()**, **fsprintf()**.

#include <stdio.h>
int sscanf(char *buf, const char *format, arg_list)

The **sscanf()** function is identical to **scanf()**, except data is read from the array pointed to by *buf* rather than **stdin**.

The return value is equal to the number of fields that were actually assigned values. This number does not include fields that were skipped through the use of the * format command modifier. A value of 0 means that no fields were assigned, and EOF indicates that a read was attempted at the end of the string.

Related functions: **scanf()**, **fscanf()**.

#include <io.h>
long int tell(int fd)

The **tell()** function is part of the UNIX-like I/O system and is not defined by the ANSI standard. It returns the current value of the file position indicator associated with the file descriptor **fd**. This value will be the number of bytes the position indicator is from the start of the file. A return value of -1L indicates an error.

Related functions: **lseek()**, **open()**, **close()**, **read()**, **write()**.

#include <stdio.h>
char *tmpnam(char *name)

The **tmpnam()** function generates a unique filename and stores it in the array pointed to by *name*. The main purpose of **tmpnam()** is to generate a temporary filename that is different from any other file in the directory.

The function may be called up to a number of times equal to **TMP_MAX**, defined in **stdio.h**. Each time, it will generate a new temporary filename.

A pointer to *name* is returned on success; otherwise, a null pointer is returned.

Related function: **tmpfile()**.

#include <stdio.h>
FILE *tmpfile(void)

The **tmpfile()** function opens a temporary file for update and returns a pointer to the stream or a null pointer on failure. The function automatically uses a unique filename to avoid conflicts with existing files.

The temporary file created by **tmpfile()** is automatically removed when the file is closed or when the program terminates.

Related function: **tmpnam()**.

#include <stdio.h>
int ungetc(int ch, FILE *stream)

The **ungetc()** function returns the character specified by the low-order byte of *ch* back onto the input stream *stream*. This character will then be returned by the next read operation on *stream*. A call to **fflush()** or **fseek()** undoes an **ungetc()** operation and discards the character that was put back.

You may not unget an EOF.

A call to **ungetc()** clears the end-of-file flag associated with the specified stream. The value of the file position indicator for a text stream is undefined until all pushed-back characters are read, in which case it will be the same as it was prior to the first **ungetc()** call. For binary streams, each **ungetc()** call decrements the file position indicator.

The return value is equal to *ch* on success and EOF on failure.

Related function: **getc()**.

#include <stdio.h>
int unlink(const char *fname)

The **unlink()** function is part of the UNIX-like I/O system and is not defined by the proposed ANSI standard. It removes the specified file from the directory. It returns 0 on success and a -1 on failure.

Related functions: **open()**, **close()**.

```
#include <stdio.h>
int vprintf(const char *format,
        va_list arg_ptr)
int vfprintf(FILE *stream, const char
        *format, va_list arg_ptr)
int vsprintf(char *buf, const char *format,
        va_list arg_ptr)
int vscanf(const char *format,
        va_list arg_ptr)
int vfscanf(FILE *stream, const char
        *format, va_list arg_ptr)
int vsscanf(char *str, const char *format,
        va_list arg_ptr)
```

The functions **vprintf()**, **vfprintf()**, and **vsprintf()** are functionally equivalent to **printf()**, **fprintf()**, and **sprintf()**, respectively, except that the argument list has been replaced by a pointer to a list of arguments. This pointer must be of type **va_list** and is defined in **stdarg.h**.

The functions **vscanf()**, **vfscanf()**, and **vsscanf()** are functionally equivalent to **scanf()**, **fscanf()**, and **sscanf()**, respectively, except that the argument list has been replaced by a pointer to a list of arguments. This pointer must be of type **va_list** and is defined in **stdarg.h**.

Related functions: **va_list()**, **va_start()**, **va_end()**.

#include <io.h>
int write(int fd, void *buf, unsigned count)

The **write()** function is part of the UNIX-like I/O system and is not defined by the proposed ANSI standard. It writes *count* number of bytes to the file described by *fd* from the buffer pointed to by *buf*. The file position indicator is adjusted forward by the number of bytes written. If the file is opened in text mode, then character translations may take place.

The return value will be equal to the number of bytes actually written. This number may be smaller than *count* if an error is encountered. A return value of -1 means an error has occurred.

Related functions: **read()**, **close()**, **write()**, **lseek()**.

STRING AND CHARACTER FUNCTIONS

The Turbo C library has a rich and varied set of string- and character-handling functions. In C, a string is a null-terminated array of characters. The prototypes to the string functions are in the header file **strings.h**. The character functions use **ctype.h** as their header file. The memory manipulation functions have their prototypes in both **string.h** and **mem.h**.

Because C has no bounds checking on array operations, it is your responsibility to prevent an array overflow. As the ANSI committee puts it, if an array has overflowed, "the behavior is undefined," which is a nice way of saying that your program is about to crash!

In Turbo C, a *printable character* is one that can be displayed on a terminal. These are the characters between a space

(0x20) and tilde (0xFE). Control characters and the DEL key have values between 0 and 0x1F.

The character functions are declared to take an integer argument. While this is true, only the low-order byte is used by the function. Generally, you are free to use a character argument because it will automatically be elevated to **int** at the time of the call.

Many of the functions take arguments of type **size_t**, which is defined as an unsigned integer.

#include <ctype.h>
int isalnum(int ch)

The **isalnum()** function returns a nonzero value if its argument is either a letter of the alphabet or a digit. If the character is not alphanumeric, then 0 is returned.

Related functions: **isalpha()**, **isdigit()**, **iscntrl()**, **isgraph()**, **isprint()**, **ispunct()**, **isspace()**.

#include <ctype.h>
int isalpha(int ch)

The **isalpha()** function returns a nonzero value if *ch* is a letter of the alphabet; otherwise, 0 is returned.

Related functions: **isalnum()**, **isdigit()**, **iscntrl()**, **isgraph()**, **isprint()**, **ispunct()**, **isspace()**.

#include <ctype.h>
int iscntrl(int ch)

The **iscntrl()** function returns a nonzero value if *ch* is a control character; otherwise, 0 is returned.

Related functions: **isalnum()**, **isdigit()**, **isalpha()**, **isgraph()**, **isprint()**, **ispunct()**, **isspace()**.

#include <ctype.h>
int isdigit(int ch)

The **isdigit()** function returns a nonzero value if *ch* is a digit from 0 through 9. Otherwise, 0 is returned.

Related functions: **isalnum()**, **iscntrl()**, **isalpha()**, **isgraph()**, **isprint()**, **ispunct()**, **isspace()**.

#include <ctype.h>
int isgraph(int ch)

The **isgraph()** function returns a nonzero value if *ch* is any printable character other than a space; otherwise, 0 is returned.

Related functions: **isalnum()**, **iscntrl()**, **isalpha()**, **isdigit()**, **isprint()**, **ispunct()**, **isspace()**.

#include <ctype.h>
int islower(int ch)

The **islower()** function returns a nonzero value if *ch* is a lowercase letter; otherwise, 0 is returned.

Related function: **isupper()**.

#include <ctype.h>
int isprint(int ch)

The **isprint()** function returns a nonzero value if *ch* is a printable character, including a space; otherwise, 0 is returned. Although implementation dependent, printable characters are often in the range 0x20 through 0x7E.

Related functions: **isalnum(), iscntrl(), isalpha(), isdigit(), isgraph(), ispunct(), isspace().**

#include <ctype.h>
int ispunct(int ch)

The **ispunct()** function returns a nonzero value if *ch* is a punctuation character, excluding the space; otherwise, 0 is returned. The term "punctuation," for the purposes of this function, is defined as all printing characters that are neither alphanumeric nor white space.

Related functions: **isalnum(), iscntrl(), isalpha(), isdigit(), isgraph(), ispunct(), isspace().**

#include <ctype.h>
int isspace(int ch)

The **isspace()** function returns a nonzero value if *ch* is either a space, tab, or newline character; otherwise, 0 is returned.

Related functions: **isalnum(), iscntrl(), isalpha(), isdigit(), isgraph(), isspace(), ispunct().**

#include <ctype.h>
int isupper(int ch)

The **isupper()** function returns a nonzero value if *ch* is an uppercase letter; otherwise, 0 is returned.

Related function: **islower().**

#include <ctype.h>
int isxdigit(int ch)

The **isxdigit()** function returns a nonzero value if *ch* is a hexadecimal digit; otherwise, 0 is returned. A hexadecimal digit will be in one of these ranges: A-F, a-f, or 0-9.

Related functions: **isalnum(), iscntrl(), isalpha(), isdigit(), isgraph(), isspace(), ispunct().**

#include <string.h>
void *memchr(const void *buffer, int ch, size_t count)

The **memchr()** function searches *buffer* for the first occurrence of *ch* in the first *count* characters. It returns a pointer to the first occurrence of *ch* in *buffer* or a null pointer if *ch* is not found.

Related functions: **memmove(),memcpy().**

#include <string.h>
int memcmp(const void *buf1, const void *buf2, size_t count)
int memicmp(const void *buf1, const void *buf2, size_t count)

The **memcmp()** function compares the first *count* characters of the arrays pointed to by *buf1* and *buf2*. The comparison is done lexicographically.

The **memcmp()** function returns an integer that is interpreted as indicated here:

Value	Meaning
Less than 0	*buf1* is less than *buf2*
0	*buf1* is equal to *buf2*
Greater than 0	*buf1* is greater than *buf2*

The **memicmp()** function is the same as **memcmp()**, except that case is ignored.

Related functions: **memcpy()**, **memchr()**, **strcmp()**.

```
#include <string.h>
void *memcpy(void *to, const void *from,
       size_t count)
void *memccpy(void *to, const void *from,
       int ch, size_t count)
```

The **memcpy()** function copies *count* characters from the array pointed to by *from* into the array pointed to by *to*. It returns a pointer to *to*.

The **memccpy()** function copies up to *count* characters from *from* into *to*, stopping when the first character equal to *ch* is copied. It returns a pointer to *to*.

Related function: **memmove()**.

```
#include <string.h>
void *memmove(void *to, const void
       *from, size_t count)
```

The **memmove()** function copies *count* characters from the array pointed to by *from* into the array pointed to by *to*. The **memmove()** function returns a pointer to *to*.

Related function: **memcpy()**.

#include <string.h>
► **void *memset(void *buf, int ch, size_t count)**

The **memset()** function copies the low-order byte of *ch* into the first *count* characters of the array pointed to by *buf*. It returns *buf*. The most common use of **memset()** is to initialize a region of memory to some known value.

Related functions: **memcpy()**, **memcmp()**, **memmove()**.

#include <string.h>
► **char *strcat(char *str1, const char *str2)**

The **strcat()** function concatenates a copy of *str2* to *str1* and terminates *str1* with a null. The null terminator originally ending *str1* is overwritten by the first character of *str2*. The string *str2* is untouched by the operation. The **strcat()** function returns *str1*.

Remember, no bounds checking takes place, so it is the programmer's responsibility to ensure *str1* is large enough to hold both its original contents and those of *str2*.

Related functions: **strchr()**, **strcmp()**, **strcpy()**.

#include <string.h>
► **char *strchr(const char *str, int ch)**

The **strchr()** function returns a pointer to the first occurrence of the low-order byte of *ch* in the string pointed to by *str*. If no match is found, a null pointer is returned.

Related functions: **strpbrk()**, **strstr()**, **strtok()**, **strspn()**.

#include <string.h>
int strcmp(const char *str1, const char *str2)

The **strcmp()** function lexicographically compares two null-terminated strings and returns an integer based on the outcome, as shown here:

Value	Meaning
Less than 0	*str1* is less than *str2*
0	*str1* is equal to *str2*
Greater than 0	*str1* is greater than *str2*

Related functions: **strchr()**, **strcmp()**, **strcpy()**, **strncmp()**.

#include <string.h>
char *strcpy(char *str1, const char *str2)

The **strcpy()** function is used to copy the contents of *str2* into *str1*. The string *str2* must be a pointer to a null-terminated string. The **strcpy()** function returns a pointer to *str1*.

Related functions: **strchr()**, **strcmp()**, **memcpy()**, **strncmp()**.

#include <string.h>
int strcspn(const char *str1, const char *str2)

The **strcspn()** function returns the index of the first character in the string pointed to by *str1* that matches any of the characters in the string pointed to by *str2*.

Related functions: **strpbrk()**, **strstr()**, **strtok()**, **strrchr()**.

#include <string.h>
char *strerror(int err) char *_strerror (const char *err)

The **strerror()** function generates a string that corresponds to an explanation associated with the error number *err*. It returns a pointer to the string.

The **_strerror()** function generates a custom error message by combining *err* and the string associated with the last error generated by the system.

#include <string.h>
size_t strlen(const char *str)

The **strlen()** function returns the length of the null-terminated string pointed to by *str*. The null is not counted.

Related functions: **strchr()**, **strcmp()**, **memcpy()**, **strncmp()**.

#include <string.h>
char *strncat(char *str1, const char *str2, size_t count)

The **strncat()** function concatenates no more than *count* characters of the string pointed to by *str2* to the string pointed to by *str1* and terminates *str1* with a null. The null terminator originally ending *str1* is overwritten by the first character of *str2*. The string *str2* is untouched by the operation. The **strncat()** function returns *str1*.

Remember, no bounds checking takes place, so it is the programmer's responsibility to ensure *str1* is large enough to hold both its original contents and those of *str2*.

Related functions: **strnchr()**, **strncmp()**, **strncpy()**, **strcat()**.

#include <string.h>
int strncmp(const char *str1, const char *str2, size_t count)

The **strncmp()** function lexicographically compares no more than *count* characters from the two null-terminated strings and returns an integer based on the outcome, as shown here:

Value	**Meaning**
Less than 0	*str1* is less than *str2*
0	*str1* is equal to *str2*
Greater than 0	*str1* is greater than *str2*

If there are less than *count* characters in either string, then the comparison ends when the first null is encountered.

Related functions: **strnchr()**, **strcmp()**, **strncpy()**.

#include <string.h>
char *strncpy(char *str1, const char *str2, size_t count)

The **strncpy()** function is used to copy up to *count* characters from the string pointed to by *str2* into the string pointed to by *str1*. The string *str2* must be a pointer to a null-terminated string. The **strncpy()** function returns a pointer to *str1*.

If the string pointed to by *str2* has less than *count* characters, then nulls will be appended to the end of *str1* until *count* characters have been copied. If the string pointed to by *str2* is longer than *count* characters, then the resultant string pointed to by *str1* will not be null terminated.

Related functions: **strchr()**, **strncmp()**, **memcpy()**, **strncat()**.

```
#include <string.h>
char *strpbrk(const char *str1,
        const char *str2)
```

The **strpbrk()** function returns a pointer to the first character in the string pointed to by *str1* that matches any character in the string pointed to by *str2*. The null terminators are not included. If there are no matches, a null pointer is returned.

Related functions: **strrchr()**, **strstr()**, **strtok()**, **strspn()**.

```
#include <string.h>
char *strrchr(const char *str, int ch)
```

The **strrchr()** function returns a pointer to the last occurrence of the low-order byte of *ch* in the string pointed to by *str*. If no match is found, a null pointer is returned.

Related functions: **strpbrk()**, **strstr()**, **strtok()**, **strspn()**.

```
#include <string.h>
int strspn(const char *str1,
        const char *str2)
```

The **strspn()** function returns the index of the first character in the string pointed to by *str1* that does not match any of the characters in the string pointed to by *str2*.

Related functions: **strpbrk()**, **strstr()**, **strtok()**, **strrchr()**.

#include <string.h>
► char *strstr(const char *str1, const char *str2)

The **strstr()** function returns a pointer to the first occurrence in the string pointed to by *str1* of the string pointed to by *str2* (except the null terminator in *str2*). It returns a null pointer if no match is found.

Related functions: **strpbrk()**, **strspn()**, **strtok()**, **strchr()**, **strrchr()**, **strcspn()**.

#include <string.h>
► char *strtok(char *str1, const char *str2)

The **strtok()** function returns a pointer to the next token in the string pointed to by *str1*. The characters making up the string pointed to by *str2* are the delimiters that determine the token. A null pointer is returned when there is no token to return.

The first time **strtok()** is called, *str1* is actually used in the call. Subsequent calls use a null pointer for the first argument. In this way the entire string can be reduced to its tokens.

It is important to understand that the **strtok()** function modifies the string pointed to by *str1*. Each time a token is found, a null is placed where the delimiter was found. In this way **strtok()** can continue to advance through the string.

It is possible to use a different set of delimiters for each call to **strtok()**.

Related functions: **strpbrk()**, **strspn()**, **strtok()**, **strchr()**, **strrchr()**, **strcspn()**.

#include <ctype.h>
int tolower(int ch)

The **tolower()** function returns the lowercase equivalent of *ch* if *ch* is a letter; otherwise, *ch* is returned unchanged.

Related function: **toupper()**.

#include <ctype.h>
int toupper(int ch)

The **toupper()** function returns the uppercase equivalent of *ch* if *ch* is a letter; otherwise, *ch* is returned unchanged.

Related function: **tolower()**.

MATHEMATICAL FUNCTIONS

Turbo C includes several mathematical functions that take **double** arguments and return **double** values. These functions fall into the following categories:

- Trigonometric functions
- Hyperbolic functions
- Exponential and logarithmic functions
- Miscellaneous functions

The header **math.h** must be included in any program that uses the math functions. In addition to declaring the math functions, this header defines three macros called **EDOM**, **ERANGE**, and **HUGE_VAL**. If an argument to a math function is not in the domain for which it is defined, then the global variable **errno** is set equal to **EDOM**. If a routine produces a result that is too large to be represented by a **double**, an overflow occurs. This causes the routine to return **HUGE_VAL** and **errno** is set to **ERANGE**, indicating a range error. If an underflow happens, the routine returns 0 and sets **errno** to **ERANGE**.

#include <math.h>
double acos(double arg)

The **acos()** function returns the arc cosine of *arg*. The argument to **acos()** must be in the range -1 to 1; otherwise, a domain error will occur.

Related functions: **asin()**, **atan()**, **atan2()**, **sin()**, **cos()**, **tan()**, **sinh()**, **cosh()**, **tanh()**.

#include <math.h>
double asin(double arg)

The **asin()** function returns the arc sine of *arg*. The argument to **asin()** must be in the range -1 to 1; otherwise, a domain error will occur.

Related functions: **asin()**, **atan()**, **atan2()**, **sin()**, **cos()**, **tan()**, **sinh()**, **cosh()**, **tanh()**.

#include <math.h>
double atan(double arg)

The **atan()** function returns the arc tangent of *arg*.

Related functions: **asin()**, **acos()**, **atan2()**, **tan()**, **cos()**, **sin()**, **sinh()**, **cosh()**, **tanh()**.

#include <math.h>
► double atan2(doubel y, double x)

The **atan2()** function returns the arc tangent of *y/x*. It uses the signs of its arguments to compute the quadrand of the return value.

Related functions: **asin()**, **acos()**, **atan()**, **tan()**, **cos()**, **sin()**, **sinh()**, **cosh()**, **tanh()**.

#include <math.h>
► double ceil(double num)

The **ceil()** function returns the smallest integer (represented as a **double**) not less than *num*. For example, given 1.02, **ceil()** would return 2.0. Given -1.02, **ceil()** would return -1.

Related functions: **floor()**, **fmod()**.

#include <math.h>
► double cos(double arg)

The **cos()** function returns the cosine of *arg*. The value of *arg* must be in radians.

Related functions: **asin()**, **acos()**, **atan2()**, **atan()**, **tan()**, **sin()**, **sinh()**, **cosh()**, **tanh()**.

#include <math.h>
► double cosh(double arg)

The **cosh()** function returns the hyperbolic cosine of *arg*. The value of *arg* must be in radians.

Related functions: **asin()**, **acos()**, **atan2()**, **atan()**, **tan()**, **sin()**, **cosh()**, **tanh()**.

#include <math.h>
double exp(double arg)

The **exp()** function returns the natural logarithm *e* raised to the *arg* power.

Related function: **log()**.

#include <math.h>
double fabs(double num)

The **fabs()** function returns the absolute value of *num*.

Related function: **abs()**.

#include <math.h>
double floor(double num)

The **floor()** function returns the largest integer (represented as a double) not greater than *num*. For example, given 1.02, **floor()** would return 1.0, and given -1.02, **floor()** would return a value of -2.0.

Related functions: **fceil()**, **fmod()**.

#include <math.h>
double fmod(double x, double y)

The **fmod()** function returns the remainder of *x*/*y*.

Related functions: **ceil()**, **floor()**, **fabs()**.

#include <math.h>
double frexp(double num, int *exp)

The **frexp()** function decomposes the number *num* into a mantissa in the range 0.5 to less than 1, and an integer exponent such that $num=mantissa*2^{exp}$. The mantissa is returned by the function and the exponent is stored at the variable pointed to by *exp*.

Related function: **ldexp()**.

#include <math.h>
double ldexp(double num, int exp)

The **ldexp()** returns the value of $num * 2^{exp}$. If overflow occurs, **HUGE_VAL** is returned.

Related functions: **frexp()**, **modf()**.

#include <math.h>
double log(double num)

The **log()** function returns the natural logarithm for *num*. A domain error occurs if *num* is negative, and a range error occurs if the argument is 0.

Related function: **log10()**.

#include <math.h>
double log10(double num)

The **log10()** function returns the base 10 logarithm for *num*. A domain error occurs if *num* is negative, and a range error occurs if the argument is 0.

Related function: **log()**.

#include <math.h>
double modf(double num, double *i)

The **modf()** function breaks down *num* into its integer and fractional parts. It returns the fractional portion and places the integer part in the variable pointed to by *i*.

Related functions: **frexp()**, **ldexp()**.

#include <math.h>
double pow(double base, double exp)

The **pow()** function returns *base* raised to the *exp* power ($base^{exp}$). A domain error occurs if *base* is 0 and *exp* is less than or equal to 0. It may also happen if *base* is negative and *exp* is not an integer. An overflow produces a range error.

Related functions: **exp()**, **log()**, **sqrt()**.

#include <math.h>
double sin(double arg)

The **sin()** function returns the sine of *arg*. The value of *arg* must be in radians.

Related functions: **asin()**, **acos()**, **atan2()**, **atan()**, **tan()**, **cos()**, **sinh()**, **cosh()**, **tanh()**.

#include <math.h>
double sinh(double arg)

The **sinh()** function returns the hyperbolic sine of *arg*. The value of *arg* must be in radians.

Related functions: **asin()**, **acos()**, **atan2()**, **atan()**, **tan()**, **cos()**, **tanh()**, **cosh()**.

#include <math.h>
► double sqrt(double num)

The **sqrt()** function returns the square root of *num*. If called with a negative argument, a domain error will occur.

Related functions: **exp()**, **log()**, **pow()**.

#include <math.h>
► double tan(double arg)

The **tan()** function returns the tangent of *arg*. The value of *arg* must be in radians.

Related functions: **asin()**, **atan()**, **atan2()**, **atan()**, **cos()**, **sin()**, **sinh()**, **cosh()**, **tanh()**.

#include <math.h>
► double tanh(double arg)

The **tanh()** function returns the hyperbolic tangent of *arg*. The value of *arg* must be in radians.

Related functions: **asin()**, **atan()**, **atan2()**, **atan()**, **cos()**, **sin()**, **cosh()**, **sin()**.

DYNAMIC ALLOCATION

Turbo C has a wide variety of dynamic allocation functions that will satisfy any programming need.

The proposed ANSI standard specifies that the header information necessary to the dynamic allocation system will be in **stdlib.h**. Turbo C does put the prototypes to those allocation functions that are defined by ANSI into this header.

However, those functions not defined by ANSI have their prototypes in the **alloc.h** file.

The proposed ANSI standard only defines four functions for the dynamic allocation system: **calloc()**, **malloc()**, **free()**, and **realloc()**. However, Turbo C supplies several others that are in wide use. Some of these additional functions are necessary to efficiently support the segmented architecture of the 8086 family of processors.

The **size_t** type is used in several of the prototypes for the allocation functions and is essentially equivalent to an unsigned integer.

#include <stdlib.h>
► void *calloc(size_t num, size_t size)

The **calloc()** function returns a pointer to the allocated memory. The amount of memory allocated is equal to *num**size*. That is, **calloc()** allocates sufficient memory for an array of *num* objects of size *size*.

The **calloc()** function returns a pointer to the first byte of the allocated region. If there is not enough memory to satisfy the request, a null pointer is returned. It is always important to verify that the return value is not a null pointer before attempting to use it.

Related functions: **malloc()**, **realloc()**, **free()**.

```
#include alloc.h>
unsigned coreleft()  /* For small data
        models */
unsigned long coreleft()  /* For large data
        models */
```

The **coreleft()** function returns the approximate number of free bytes left in the heap.

Related function: **malloc()**.

```
#include <alloc.h>
void farfree(void far *ptr)
```

The **farfree()** function returns to the system the memory pointed to by the **far** pointer *ptr*. This makes the memory available for future allocation.

It is imperative that **farfree()** only be called with a pointer that was previously allocated using **farmalloc()**—it cannot free pointers allocated by other allocation functions. Using an invalid pointer in the call will probably destroy the memory management mechanism and cause a system crash.

Related functions: **farmalloc()**, **realloc()**, **calloc()**.

```
#include <alloc.h>
void far *farmalloc(size_t size)
```

The **farmalloc()** function returns a far pointer to the first byte of a region of memory of size *size* that has been allocated from outside the default data segment. If there is insufficient memory to satisfy the request, **farmalloc()** returns a null pointer. It is always important to verify that the return value is not a null pointer before attempting to use it.

Related functions: **farfree()**, **realloc()**, **calloc()**.

#include <stdlib.h>
▶ void free(void *ptr)

The **free()** function returns the memory pointed to by *ptr* back to the heap. This makes the memory available for future allocation.

It is imperative that **free()** only be called with a pointer that was previously allocated with one of the dynamic allocation system's functions, such as **malloc()** or **calloc()**. Using an invalid pointer in the call will probably destroy the memory management mechanism and cause a system crash.

Related functions: **malloc()**, **realloc()**, **calloc()**.

#include <stdlib.h>
▶ void *malloc(size_t size)

The **malloc()** function returns a pointer to the first byte of a region of memory of size *size* that has been allocated from the heap. If there is insufficient memory in the heap to satisfy the request, **malloc()** returns a null pointer. It is always important to verify that the return value is not a null pointer before attempting to use it; attempting to use a null pointer will usually result in a system crash.

Related functions: **free()**, **realloc()**, **calloc()**.

#include <stdlib.h>
▶ void *realloc(void *ptr, void *size)

The **realloc()** function changes the size of the allocated memory pointed to by *ptr* to that specified by *size*. The value of *size*. The value of *size* may be greater or less than the original. A pointer to the memory block is returned because it may be necessary for **realloc()** to move the block in order to increase its size. If this occurs, the contents of the old block are copied into the new block, and no information is lost.

Related functions: **free()**, **malloc()**, **calloc()**.

TEXT SCREEN AND GRAPHICS FUNCTIONS

The proposed ANSI standard does not define any text screen or graphics functions, mainly because the capabilities of diverse hardware environments preclude standardization across a wide range of machines. However, Turbo C provides extensive screen and graphics support systems for the PC environment. If you will not be porting your code to a different computer system, you should feel free to use them—they can enhance any application. In fact, intensive screen control is a must for most successful commercial programs.

The prototypes and header information for the text screen handling functions are in **conio.h**. The prototypes and related information for the graphics system is in **graphics.h**. The graphics system requires that the **graphics.lib** library be linked with your program.

A key factor in both text screen manipulation and graphics functions is the *window*. A window is the active part of the screen within which output is displayed. A window can be as large as the entire screen (as it is by default), or it can be as small as you require.

Turbo C uses different terminology when referring to windows in text screen and graphics systems. The text screen functions refer to windows, but a window is called a *viewport* in the graphics system; however, the concept is the same. There is also a slight difference in screen orientation. When the screen is in text mode, the upper-left corner is located at 1,1; however, in a graphics mode, this location is 0,0.

It is important to understand that most screen and graphics functions are window, or viewport, relative. For example, the **gotoxy()** text screen cursor location function sends the cursor to the specified x,y position in relation to the window, not in relation to the screen.

Keep in mind that all graphics functions are **far** functions.

#include <graphics.h>
void far arc(int x, int y, int start, int end, int radius)

The **arc()** function draws an arc from *start* to *end* (these are in degrees) along an invisible circle with a center of *x,y* and a radius of *radius*. The color of the arc is determined by the current drawing color.

Related functions: **circle()**, **ellipse()**, **getarccoords()**.

#include <graphics.h>
void far bar(int left, int top, int right, int bottom)
void far bar3d(int left, int top, int right, int bottom, int depth, int topflag)

The **bar()** function draws a rectangular bar. Its upper-left corner is defined by *left* and *top*, and its lower-right corner is defined by *right* and *bottom*. The bar is filled with the current fill pattern and color and is not outlined.

The **bar3d()** function is the same as **bar()** except it produces a three-dimensional bar of *depth* pixels deep, and the bar is outlined in the current drawing color. This means that if you want a two-dimensional outlined bar, use **bar3d()** with a depth of zero. If the *topflag* is a nonzero value, a top will be added to the bar; otherwise, the bar will not have a top.

Related function: **rectangle()**.

```
#include <graphics.h>
void far circle(int x, int y, int radius)
```

The **circle()** function draws a circle in the current drawing color with a center at *x,y* and a radius, in pixels, of *radius*.

Related functions: **arc()**, **ellipse()**.

```
#include <graphics.h>
void far cleardevice(void)
void far clearviewport(void)
```

The **cleardevice()** function clears the screen and resets the current position to 0,0. This function is used only with the graphics screen modes.

The **clearviewport()** function clears the current viewport and resets the current position to 0,0. After **clearviewport()** has executed, the viewport no longer exists.

Related function: **getviewsettings()**.

#include <graphics.h>
void far closegraph(void)

The **closegraph()** functon deactivates the graphics environment, which includes returning to the system the memory that was used to hold the graphics drivers and fonts. This function should be used when your program uses both graphics and nongraphics output. It will also return the system video mode to what it was prior to the call to **initgraph()**.

You may use **restorecrtmode()** in place of **closegraph()** if your program is terminating. In this case, any allocated memory is freed automatically.

Related function: **initgraph()**.

#include <conio.h>
void clreol(void)
void clrscr(void)

The **clreol()** function clears the screen from the current cursor position to the end of the line in the active text window. The cursor position remains unchanged.

The **clrscr()** function clears the entire active text window and locates the cursor in the upper-left corner (1,1).

Related functions: **delline()**, **window()**.

#include <conio.h>
int cputs(const char *str)

The **cputs()** function outputs the string pointed to by *str* to the current text window. Its output may not be redirected, and it automatically prevents the boundaries of the window from being overrun. It returns the last character written if successful and EOF on failure.

Related functions: **cprintf()**, **window()**.

#include <conio.h>
► void delline(void)

The **delline()** function deletes the line in the active window that contains the cursor. All lines below the deleted line are moved up to fill the void. If the current window is smaller than the entire screen, only the text that is inside the window is affected.

Related functions: **clreol()**, **insline()**.

#include <graphics.h>
► void far detectgraph(int far *driver, int far *mode)

The **detectgraph()** function determines what type of graphics adapter, if any, the computer contains. If the system does have a graphics adapter, **detectgraph()** returns the number of the appropriate graphics driver for the adapter in the integer pointed to by *driver*. It sets the variable pointed to by *mode* to the highest resolution supported by the adapter. If no graphics hardware is in the system, the variable pointed to by *driver* will contain -2. The IBM 8514 adapter cannot be properly autodetected.

Related functions: **initgraph()**.

#include <graphics.h>
void far drawpoly(int numpoints, int far *points)

The **drawpoly()** function draws a polygon with the current drawing color. The number of end points in the polygon is equal to *numpoints*. Because each point consists of both and x and y coordinates, the integer array pointed to by *points* must be at least as large as two times the number of points.

Related functions: **fillpoly()**, **line()**, **circle()**.

#include <graphics.h>
void far ellipse(int x, int y, int start, int end, int xradius, int yradius)

The **ellipse()** function draws an ellipse in the current drawing color. The center of the ellipse is at *x,y*. The length of the x and y radiuses are specified by *xradius* and *yradius*. The values for *start* and *end*, which are specified in degrees, determine how much of the drawn ellipse is displayed. If *start* equals 0 and *end* equals 360, the entire ellipse is shown.

Related functions: **circle()**, **arc()**.

#include <graphics.h>
void far fillpoly(int numpoints, int far *points)

The **fillpoly()** function first uses the current drawing color to draw an object that consists of *numpoints* points defined by the x,y coordinates in the array pointed to by *points*. (See **drawpoly()** for details on the construction of a polygon.) It then proceeds to fill the object with the current fill pattern and color. The fill pattern can be set by calling **setfillpattern()**.

Related function: **floodfill()**.

#include <graphics.h>
void far floodfill(int x, int y, int border)

The **floodfill()** function fills an object with the current fill color and pattern, given the coordinates of any point within that object and the color of its border (that is, the color of the lines or arcs that make up the object). The object being filled must be completely enclosed, or else the area outside of the shape will be filled as well. The function does not work with the IBM 8514 adapter.

Related function: **fillpoly()**.

#include <graphics.h>
void far getarccoords(struct arccoordstype far *coords)

The **getarccoords()** function fills the structure pointed to by *coords* with coordinates related to the last call to **arc()**. The *arccoordstype* structure is defined as

```
struct arccoordstype {
  int x, y;
  int xstart, ystart, xend, yend;
};
```

Here **x** and **y** are the center of the imaginary circle about which the arc was drawn. The starting and ending x,y coordinates are stored in *xstart, ystart* and *xend, yend.*

Related functions: **line()**, **pieslice()**.

```
#include <graphics.h>
void far getaspectratio(int far *xasp,
        int far *yasp)
```

The **getaspectratio()** function copies the x aspect ratio into the variable pointed to by *xasp* and the y aspect ratio into the variable pointed to by *yasp*. You can manipulate these aspect ratios to alter the way objects are displayed on the screen.

Related functions: **circle()**, **ellipse()**, **arc()**.

```
#include <graphics.h>
int far getbkcolor(void)
```

The **getbkcolor()** function returns the integer equivalent of the current background color. The values and their corresponding macros (defined in **graphics.h**) are shown here:

Value	Macro
0	BLACK
1	BLUE
2	GREEN
3	CYAN
4	RED
5	MAGENTA
6	BROWN
7	LIGHTGRAY
8	DARKGRAY
9	LIGHTBLUE
10	LIGHTGREEN

Value	Macro
11	LIGHTCYAN
12	LIGHTRED
13	LIGHTMAGENTA
14	YELLOW
15	WHITE

Related function: **setbkcolor()**.

#include <graphics.h>
int far getcolor(void)

The **getcolor()** function returns the current drawing color.

Related function: **setcolor()**.

#include <graphics.h>
void far getfillpattern(char far *pattern)

The **getfillpattern()** function fills the array pointed to by *pattern* with the eight bytes that comprise the current fill pattern. The array must be at least eight bytes long. The pattern is arranged as an eight-bit by eight-byte pattern.

Related functions: **setfillpattern()**, **setfillstyle()**.

#include <graphics.h>
void far getfillsettings (struct fillsettingstype far *info)

The **getfillsettings()** function fills the structure pointed to by *info* with the number of the fill pattern and with the color currently in use. The *fillsettingstype* structure is defined in **graphics.h** as

```
struct fillsettingstype {
  int pattern;
  int color;
};
```

The values for *pattern* are shown here, along with their macro equivalents (defined in **graphics.h**):

Value	**Macro**	**Meaning**
0	**EMPTY_FILL**	Fill with background color
1	**SOLID_FILL**	Fill with solid color
2	**LINE_FILL**	Fill with lines
3	**LTSLASH_FILL**	Fill with light slashes
4	**SLASH_FILL**	Fill with slashes
5	**BKSLASH_FILL**	Fill with backslashes
6	**LTBKSLASH_FILL**	Fill with light backslashes
8	**XHATCH_FILL**	Fill with hatching
9	**INTERLEAVE_FILL**	Fill with interleaving
10	**WIDE_DOT_FILL**	Fill with widely spaced dots
11	**CLOSE_DOT_FILL**	Fill with closely spaced dots
12	**USER_FILL**	Fill with custom pattern

The color will be one of the colors that is valid in the video mode currently in use.

Related function: **setfillsettings()**.

#include <graphics.h>
int far getgraphmode(void)

The **getgraphmode()** function returns the current graphics mode. The value returned does *not* correspond to the actual value that BIOS associates with the active video mode. Instead, the value is relative to the current video driver and is defined in **graphics.h**. Here is a list of values, their macro names, and resolutions:

Value	Macro	Resolution
0	CGAC0	320x200
1	CGAC1	320x200
2	CGAC2	320x200
3	CGAC3	320x200
4	CGAHI	640x200
0	MCGAC0	320x200
1	MCGAC1	320x200
2	MCGAC2	320x200
3	MCGAC3	320x200
4	MCGAMED	640x200
5	MCGAHI	640x480
0	EGALO	640x200
1	EGAHI	640x350
0	EGA64LO	640x200
1	EGA64HI	640x350
3	EGAMONOHI	640x350
0	HERCMONOHI	720x348
0	ATT400C0	320x200
1	ATT400C1	320x200
2	ATT400C2	320x200

Value	Macro	Resolution
3	ATT400C3	320x200
4	ATT400CMED	640x200
5	ATT400CHI	640x400
0	VGALO	640x200
1	VGAMED	640x350
2	VGAHI	640x480
0	PC3270HI	720x350
0	IBM8514LO	640x480
1	IBM8514HI	1024x760

Related function: **setgraphmode()**.

#include <graphics.h>
► void far getimage(int left, int top, int right, int bottom, void far *buf)

The **getimage()** function copies that portion of the graphics screen with coordinates *left,top* at the upper-left corner and coordinates *right,bottom* at the lower-right corner. The image is copied into the region of memory pointed to by *buf*.

Use the **imagesize()** function to determine the number of bytes needed to store the image. An image stored with **getimage()** can be written to the screen with the **putimage()** function.

Related functions: **putimage()**, **imagesize()**.

#include <graphics.h>
void far getlinesettings (struct linesettingstype far *info)

The **getlinesettings()** function fills the structure pointed to by *info* with the current line style. The structure *linesettingstype* is defined as

```
struct linesettingstype {
  int linestyle;
  unsigned upattern;
  int thickness;
};
```

The *linestyle* element holds the style of the line. It will be one of these enumerated values, defined in **graphics.h**:

Value	Meaning
SOLID_LINE	Unbroken line
DOTTED_LINE	Dotted line
CENTER_LINE	Centered line
DASHED_LINE	Dashed line
USERBIT_LINE	User-defined line

If *linestyle* is equal to **USERBIT_LINE**, then the 16-bit pattern in *upattern* determines how the line appears. Each bit in the pattern corresponds to one pixel. If that bit is set, the pixel is turned on; otherwise, it is turned off.

The *thickness* element will have one these values:

Value	Meaning
NORM_WIDTH	One pixel wide
THICK_WIDTH	Three pixels wide

Related function: **setlinestyle()**.

```
#include <graphics.h>
int far getmaxcolor(void)
```

The **getmaxcolor()** function returns the largest valid color value for the current video mode. For example, in four-color CGA mode the value is 3.

Related functions: **getbkcolor()**, **getpallete()**.

```
#include <graphics.h>
int far getmaxx(void)
int far getmaxy(void)
```

The **getmaxx()** function returns the largest valid x value for the current graphics mode. The **getmaxy()** function returns the largest valid y value for the current graphics mode.

Related function: **getmaxcolor()**.

```
#include <graphics.h>
void far getmoderange(int driver,
        int far  *lowmode, int far *himode)
```

The **getmoderange()** function determines the lowest and highest mode supported by the graphics driver specified by *driver* and puts these values at the variable pointed to by *low-mode* and *himode,* respectively. The valid values of *driver* are shown here, along with their macro names:

Value	Macro
1	CGA
2	MCGA
3	EGA
4	EGA64
5	EGAMONO
6	RESERVED
7	HERCMONO
8	ATT400
9	VGA
10	PC3270

Related function: **getgraphmode()**.

#include <graphics.h>
► void far getpalette(struct palettetype far *pal)

The **getpalette()** function loads the structure pointed to by *pal* with the number of the current palette. The *palettetype* structure is defined as

```
#define MAXCOLORS 15

struct palettetype {
  unsigned char size;
  signed char colors[MAXCOLORS + 1];
};
```

The *size* element holds the number of colors available in the current palette. The *colors* array holds the values for the colors available in the palette. The values for *colors* and their macro names are shown here:

CGA Codes (Background Only)

Value	Macro
0	BLACK
1	BLUE
2	GREEN
3	CYAN
4	RED
5	MAGENTA
6	BROWN
7	LIGHTGRAY
8	DARKGRAY
9	LIGHTBLUE
10	LIGHTGREEN
11	LIGHTCYAN
12	LIGHTRED
13	LIGHTMAGENTA
14	YELLOW
15	WHITE

EGA and VGA Codes

Value	Macro
0	EGA_BLACK
1	EGA_BLUE
2	EGA_GREEN
3	EGA_CYAN
4	EGA_RED
5	EGA_MAGENTA
20	EGA_BROWN
7	EGA_LIGHTGRAY

Value	Macro
56	EGA_DARKGRAY
57	EGA_LIGHTBLUE
58	EGA_LIGHTGREEN
59	EGA_LIGHTCYAN
60	LIGHTRED
61	LIGHTMAGENTA
62	EGA_YELLOW
63	EGA_WHITE

Related function: **setpalette()**.

#include <graphics.h>
int far getpixel(int x, int y)

The **getpixel()** function returns the color of the pixel located at the specified *x,y* position.

Related function: **putpixel()**.

#include <conio.h>
int gettext(int left, int top, int right, int bottom, void *buf)

The **gettext()** function copies into the buffer pointed to by *buf* the text from the rectangle that has upper-left-corner coordinates of *left* and *top* and lower-right-corner coordinates of *right* and *bottom*. The coordinates are screen, not window, relative.

The amount of memory needed to hold a region of the screen is computed by this formula:

```
num_bytes = rows x columns x 2
```

The reason for a factor of 2 is that each character displayed on the screen requires two bytes of storage: one for the character itself and the other for its attributes.

The function returns 1 on success, 0 on failure.

Related functions: **puttext()**, **movetext()**.

#include <graphics.h>
void far gettextsettings(struct textsettingstype far *info)

The **gettextsettings()** function loads the structure pointed to by *info* with information about the current graphics text settings. The structure *textsettingstype* is defined in **graphics.h** and is shown here:

```
struct textsettingstype {
  int font;      /* font type */
  int direction; /* horizontal or vertical */
  int charsize;  /* size of characters */
  int horiz;     /* horizontal justification */
  int vert;      /* vertical justification */
};
```

The *font* element will contain one of these values (as defined in **graphics.h**):

Value	Font
0	Default 8x8 bit-mapped font
1	Stroked triplex font
2	Stroked small font

Value	Font
3	Stroked sans-serif font
4	Stroked gothic font

The *direction* element must be set to either **HORIZ_DIR** (the default) for horizontal text or **VERT_DIR** for vertical text. The *charsize* element is a multiplier used to scale the size of the output text. The values in *horiz* and *vert* indicate how text will be justified in relation to the current position (CP). They will be one of the following values (the macros are defined in **graphics.h**):

Value	Macro	Meaning
0	**LEFT_TEXT**	CP at left
1	**CENTER_TEXT**	CP in the center
2	**RIGHT_TEXT**	CP at right
3	**BOTTOM_TEXT**	CP at the bottom
4	**TOP_TEXT**	CP at the top

Related function: **settextstyle()**.

#include <graphics.h>
void far getviewsettings(struct viewporttype far *info)

The **getviewsettings()** function loads information on the current viewport into the structure pointed to by *info*. The structure *viewporttype* is defined as

```
struct viewporttype {
  int left, top, right, bottom;
  int clipflag;
};
```

The fields *left, top, right,* and *bottom* hold the coordinates of the upper-left and lower-right corners of the viewport. When the value of *clipflag* is 0, the output that overruns the viewport boundaries will not be clipped. Otherwise, output will be clipped to prevent boundary overrun.

Related function: **setviewport()**.

```
#include <graphics.h>
int far getx(void)
int far gety(void)
```

The **getx()** and **gety()** functions return the x and y coordinates of the current position on the graphics screen.

Related function: **moveto()**.

```
#include <conio.h>
void gotoxy(int x, int y)
```

The **gotoxy()** function sends the text screen cursor to the location specified by *x,y*. If either or both of the coordinates are invalid, no action takes place.

Related functions: **wherex()**, **wherey()**.

```
#include <graphics.h>
void far graphdefaults(void)
```

The **graphdefaults()** function resets the graphics system to its default settings. The entire screen becomes the viewport, with the current position at 0,0. The palette, drawing color, and background color are reset. Also, the fill style and pattern, the text font, and the justification are returned to their original values.

Related functions: **initgraph()**, **setpalette()**.

#include <graphics.h>
► char far *grapherrormsg(int errcode) /*For high memory models*/
char * far grapherrormsg(int errcode) /*For all other models*/

The **grapherrormsg()** function returns a pointer to the error message that corresponds to *errcode*. The error code is obtained by a call to **graphresult()**. See **graphresult()** for details of the error conditions.

Related function: **graphresult()**.

#include <graphics.h>
► void far *far _graphgetmem(unsigned size)
void far _graphfreemem(void far *ptr, unsigned size)

The **_graphgetmem()** function is called by Turbo C's graphics system to allocate memory for graphics drivers and other graphics system needs. The **_graphfreemem()** function frees this memory.

These functions should never be called directly by your programs.

#include <graphics.h>
► int far graphresult(void)

The **graphresult()** function returns a value that represents the outcome of the last graphics operation. This value will be one of the following enumerated values:

Value	Name	Meaning
0	grOk	Successfull
-1	grNoInitGraph	No driver installed
-2	grNotDetected	No graphics hardware in system
-3	grFileNotFound	Driver file not found
-4	grInvalidDriver	Invalid driver file
-5	grNoLoadMem	Not enough memory
-6	grNoScanMem	Insufficient memory for scan fill
-7	grNoFloodMem	Insufficient memory for flood fill
-8	grFontNotFound	Font file not found
-9	grNoFontMem	Insufficient memory for font
-10	grInvalidMode	Invalid mode
-11	grError	General graphics error
-12	grIOerror	I/O error

Value	Name	Meaning
-13	grInvalidFont	Invalid font file
-14	grInvalidFontNum	Invalid font number
-15	grInvalidDeviceNum	Invalid device number

Use **grapherrormsg()** to display a graphics error message, given its error number.

Related function: **grapherrormsg()**.

#include <conio.h>
► void highvideo(void)

After a call to **highvideo()**, characters written to the screen will be displayed in high-intensity video. This function works only for text screens.

Related functions: **lowvideo()**, **normvideo()**.

#include <graphics.h>
► unsigned far imagesize(int left, int top, int right, int bottom)

The **imagesize()** function returns the number of bytes of storage necessary to hold a portion of the screen whose upper-left corner is at location *left,top* and lower-right corner is at *right,bottom*. This function is generally used in conjuction with **getimage()**.

Related function: **getimage()**.

#include <graphics.h>
**void far initgraph(int far *driver,
int far *mode, char far *path)**

The **initgraph()** function is used to initalize the graphics system and to load into memory the graphics driver that corresponds to the number pointed to by *driver*. Without a graphics driver loaded into memory, no graphics functions can operate. The *mode* parameter points to an integer that specifies the specific video mode used by the graphics functions. Finally, you may specify a path to the driver in the string pointed to by *path*. If no path is specified, the current working directory is searched.

The graphics drivers are contained in .BGI files, which must be available on the system. You need not worry about the actual name of the file, however, because you only have to specify the driver by its number. The header **graphics.h** defines these macros for that purpose.

Macro	Value
DETECT	0
CGA	1
MCGA	2
EGA	3
EGA64	4
EGAMONO	5
IBM8514	6
HERCMONO	7
ATT400	8

Macro	**Value**
VGA	9
PC3270	10

When you use the **DETECT** macro, **initgraph()** automatically detects the type of video hardware present in the system and selects the video mode with the greatest resolution.

The value of *mode* must be one of the graphics modes shown in the following table. Notice that the value pointed to by *mode* is *not* the same as the value that is recognized by the BIOS routine that actually sets the mode. Instead, the value used to call BIOS to initialize a video mode is created by **initgraph()**, using both the driver and the mode.

Driver	**Mode**	**Value**	**Resolution**
CGA	CGAC0	0	320x200
	CGAC1	1	320x200
	CGAC2	2	320x200
	CGAC3	3	320x200
	CGAHI	4	640X200
MCGA	MCGAC0	0	320x200
	MCGAC1	1	320x200
	MCGAC2	2	320x200
	MCGAC3	3	320x200
	MCGAMED	4	640x200
	MCGAHI	5	640x480
EGA	EGALO	0	640x200
	EGAHI	1	640x350
EGA64	EGA64LO	0	640x200

Driver	Mode	Value	Resolution
	EGA64HI	1	640x350
EGAMONO	EGAMONOHI	3	640x350
HERC	HERCMONOHI	0	720x348
ATT400	ATT400C0	0	320x200
	ATT400C1	1	320x200
	ATT400C2	2	320x200
	ATT400C3	3	320x200
	ATT400CMED	4	640x200
	ATT400CHI	5	640x400
VGA	VGALO	0	640x200
	VGAMED	1	640x350
	VGAHI	2	640x480
PC3270	PC3270HI	0	720x350
IBM	IBM8514LO	0	640x480
	IBM8514HI	1	1024x760

Related function: **getgraphmode()**.

#include <conio.h>
► void insline(void)

The **insline()** function inserts a blank line at the current cursor position, and all lines below the cursor move down. This function is for text mode only. It operates in relation to the current text window.

Related function: **delline()**.

#include <graphics.h>
▶ void far line(int startx, int starty, int endx, int endy)
void far lineto(int x, int y)
void far linerel(int deltax, int deltay)

The **line()** function draws a line in the current drawing color from *startx,starty* to *endx,endy*. The current position is unchanged.

The **lineto()** function draws a line in the current drawing color from the current position to *x,y,* where the current position is relocated.

The **linerel()** function draws a line from the current position to the location that is *deltax* units away in the x direction and *deltay* units away in the y direction. The current position is moved to the new location.

Related functions: **circle(), drawpoly().**

#include <conio.h>
▶ void lowvideo(void)

After a call to **lowvideo()**, characters written to the screen will be displayed in low-intensity video. This function works only for text screens.

Related functions: **highvideo(), normvideo().**

#include <graphics.h>
▶ void far moverel(int deltax, int deltay)

The **moverel()** function advances the current position on a graphics screen by the magnitudes of *deltax* and *deltay*.

Related function: **moveto().**

#include <conio.h>
int movetext(int left, int top, int right, int bottom, int newleft, int newtop);

The **movetext()** function moves the portion of a text screen whose upper-left corner is at *left,top* and lower-right corner is at *right,bottom* to the region of the screen that has *new-left,newtop* as the coordinates of its upper-left corner. This function is screen, not window, relative.

The **movetext()** function returns 0 if one or more coordinates is out of range; otherwise, 1 is returned.

Related function: **gettext()**.

#include <graphics.h>
void far moveto(int x, int y)

The **moveto()** function moves the current position to the location specified by *x,y* in relation to the current viewport. This is a graphics function that corresponds in operation to the text screen function **gotoxy()**.

Related function: **moverel()**.

#include <conio.h>
void normvideo(void)

After a call to **normvideo()**, characters written to the screen will be displayed in normal-intensity video. This function works only for text screens.

Related functions: **highvideo()**, **lowvideo()**.

```
#include <graphics.h>
void far outtext(char far *str)
void var outtextxy(int x, int y, char *str)
```

The **outtext()** function displays a text string on a graphics mode screen at the current position, using the active text settings (direction, font, size, and justification). If the active direction is horizontal, the current position is increased by the length of the string; otherwise, no change is made in the current position. In graphics modes there is no visible cursor, but the current position on the screen is maintained as if there were an invisible cursor.

To change the style of the text, refer to the **settextstyle()** function.

Related function: **settextstyle()**.

```
#include <graphics.h>
void far pieslice(int x, int y, int start,
          int  end, int radius)
```

The **pieslice()** function draws a pie slice, using the current drawing color, covering an angle equal to the value of *end* minus the value of *start*. The beginning and ending points of the angle are specified in degrees. The slice is cut from a circle with a center of *x,y* and a radius equal to *radius*. The slice is filled with the current fill pattern and color.

Related functions: **arc()**, **circle()**.

#include <graphics.h>
▶ void far putimage(int x, int y, void var *buf, int op)

The **putimage()** function copies to the screen, beginning at location *x,y,* an image previously saved with **getimage()** in the memory pointed to by *buf.* The value of *op* determines exactly how the image is written to the screen. Its valid enumerated values are as follows:

Value	Name	Meaning
0	COPY_PUT	Copy as is
1	XOR_PUT	Exclusive-OR with destination
2	OR_PUT	Inclusive-OR with destination
3	AND_PUT	AND with destination
4	NOT_PUT	Invert source image

Related functions: **getimage(), imagesize().**

#include <graphics.h>
▶ void far putpixel(int x, int y, int color)

The **putpixel()** function writes the color specified by *color* to the pixel at location *x,y.*

Related function: **getpixel().**

```
#include <conio.h>
int puttext(int left, int top, int right,
        int bottom, void *buf)
```

The **puttext()** function copies text previously saved by **gettext()** from the buffer pointed to by *buf* into the region whose upper-left and lower-right corners are specified by *left,top* and *right,bottom,* respectively.

The **puttext()** function uses screen-absolute, not window-relative, coordinates.

Related functions: **gettext()**, **movetext()**.

```
#include <graphics.h>
void far rectangle(int left, int top, int right,
        int bottom)
```

The **rectangle()** function draws a box, as defined by the coodinates *left,top* and *right,bottom,* in the current drawing color.

Related functions: **bar()**, **bar3d()**, **line()**.

```
#include <graphics.h>
int registerbgidriver(void(*driver)(void))
int registerbgifont(void (*font)(void))
```

These functions are used to notify the graphics system that a graphics driver, a font, or both have been linked in and that there is no need to look for a corresponding disk file.

You should consult the *Turbo C User's Manual* for details of the actual registration process.

#include <graphics.h>
void far restorecrtmode(void)

The **restorecrtmode()** function restores to screen to the mode in effect prior to the call to **initgraph()**.

Related function: **initgraph()**.

#include <graphics.h>
void far setactivepage(int page)

The **setactivepage()** function determines the video page that will receive the output of Turbo C's graphics functions. By default, Turbo C uses video page 0. If you call **setactivepage()** with another page, subsequent graphics output will be written to the new page, not necessarily the one currently displayed. Only the EGA and VGA graphics modes support multiple pages; however, even for these adapters, not all modes have multiple pages.

Related function: **setvisualpage()**.

#include <graphics.h>
void far setallpalette(struct palettetype far *pal)

The **setallpalette()** function is used to change all the colors in an EGA/VGA palette. The structure *palettetype* is defined as the following:

```
struct palettetype {
  unsigned char size;
  signed char colors[16];
}
```

You must set *size* equal to the number of colors in the palette and then load the color for each index into its corresponding element in the array *colors*.

Refer to **setcolor()** for the colors that are for the various adapters.

Related function: **setpalette()**.

#include <graphics.h>
► void far setbkcolor(int color)

The **setbkcolor()** function changes the background color to that specified in *color*. Valid values for *color* are shown here:

Value	Macro
0	BLACK
1	BLUE
2	GREEN
3	CYAN
4	RED
5	MAGENTA
6	BROWN
7	LIGHTGRAY
8	DARKGRAY
9	LIGHTBLUE
10	LIGHTGREEN
11	LIGHTCYAN
12	LIGHTRED
13	LIGHTMAGENTA

Number	Macro
14	YELLOW
15	WHITE

Related function: **setcolor()**.

```
#include <graphics.h>
void far setcolor(int color)
```

The **setcolor()** function sets the current drawing color as specified by *color*. For the valid colors for each video adapter, refer to **setpalette()**.

Related function: **setpalette()**.

```
#include <graphics.h>
void far setfillpattern(char far *pattern,
        int color)
```

The **setfillpattern()** function sets the fill pattern used by various functions, such as **floodfill()**, to that pointed to by *pattern*. The array must be at least eight bytes long. The pattern is arranged as an eight-bit by eight-byte pattern. When a bit is on, the color specified by *color* is displayed; otherwise, the background color is used.

Related function: **setfillstyle()**.

```
#include <graphics.h>
void far setfillstyle(int pattern, int color)
```

The **setfillstyle()** function sets the style and color of the fill used by various graphics functions. The value of *color* must be valid for the current video mode. See **getfillsettings()** for the values for *pattern,* along with their macro equivalents, defined in **graphics.h**. A custom fill pattern is defined by **setfillpattern()**.

Related function: **setfillpattern()**.

#include <graphics.h>
unsigned far setgraphbufsize(unsigned size)

The **setgraphbufsize()** function is used to set the size of the buffer used by many of the graphics functions. Generally, you will not need to use this function, if you do use it, you must call it before **initgraph()**.

Related function: **_getgraphmem()**.

#include <graphics.h>
void far setgraphmode(int mode)

The **setgraphmode()** function sets the current graphics mode as specified by *mode,* which must be a valid mode for the graphics driver.

Related function: **getmoderange()**.

include <graphics.h>
void far setlinestyle(int style, unsigned pattern, int width)

The **setlinestyle()** function sets the way a line looks when drawn with any of the graphics functions that draw lines. The *style* element holds the style of the line. It will be one of these enumerated values, defined in **graphics.h**:

Value	Meaning
SOLID_LINE	Unbroken line
DOTTED_LINE	Dotted line
CENTER_LINE	Centered line (dash-dot-dash)
DASHED_LINE	Dashed line
USERBIT_LINE	User-defined line

If *style* is equal to **USERBIT_LINE**, then the 16-bit pattern in *pattern* determines how the line appears. Each bit in the pattern corresponds to one pixel. If that bit is set, the pixel is turned on; otherwise, it is turned off.

The *thickness* element will have one of these values:

Value	Meaning
NORM_WIDTH	One pixel wide
THICK_WIDTH	Three pixels wide

The value of the *pattern* parameter is only important if the **USERBIT_LINE** is the value of *style*.

Related function: **setfillstyle()**.

#include <graphics.h>
void far setpalette(int index, int color)

The **setpalette()** function changes the colors displayed by the video system. This function's operation is somewhat complex; refer to the *Turbo C User's Manual* for details.

Related function: **setcolor()**.

#include <graphics.h>
► void far settextjustify(int horiz, int vert)

The **settextjustify()** function sets the way text will be aligned in relation to the current position (CP). The values of *horiz* and *vert* determine the effect of **settextjustify()**, as shown here (the macros are defined in **graphics.h**):

Value	Macro	Meaning
0	LEFT_TEXT	CP at left
1	CENTER_TEXT	CP in the center
2	RIGHT_TEXT	CP at right
3	BOTTOM_TEXT	CP at the bottom
4	TOP_TEXT	CP at the top

The default settings are **LEFT_TEXT** and **TOP_TEXT**.

Related function: **settextstyle()**.

#include <graphics.h>
► void far settextstyle(int font, int direction, int size)

The **settextstyle()** function sets the active font used by the graphics text output functions. It also sets the direction and size of the characters.

The *font* parameter determines the type of font used. The default is the hardware-defined 8x8 bit-mapped font. You can give *font* one of these values (the macros are defined in **graphics.h.**):

Value	Font	Meaning
0	**DEFAULT_FONT**	8x8 bit-mapped font
1	**TRIPLEX_FINT**	Stroked triplex font
2	**SMALL_FONT**	Small stroked font
3	**SANS_SERIF_FONT**	Stroked sans-serif font
4	**GOTHIC_FONT**	Stroked gothic font

The direction the text will be displayed (either left to right or bottom to top) is determined by the value of *direction*, which may be either **HORIZ_DIR** (0) or **VERT_DIR** (1).

The *charsize* parameter is a multiplier that increases the character size. It may have a value from 0 through 10.

Related function: **settextjustify()**.

#include <graphics.h>
void far setusercharsize(int mulx, int divx, int muly, int divy)

The **setusercharsize()** function is used to specify multipliers and divisors that scale the size of graphics text characters stroked fonts. In essence, after a call to **setusercharsize()**, each character displayed on the screen will have its default size multiplied by *multx/divx* for its x dimension and *muly/-divy* for its y dimension.

Related function: **gettextsettings()**.

#include <graphics.h>
void far setviewport(int left, int top, int right, int bottom, int clip)

The **setviewport()** function creates a new viewport, with upper-left and lower-right corner coordinates specified by *left,top,* and *right,bottom.* If *clip* is 1, then the output is automatically clipped at the edge of the viewport and prevented from spilling into other parts of the screen. If *clip* is 0, no clipping takes place.

Related function: **clearviewport()**.

#include <graphics.h>
void far setvisualpage(int page)

The **setvisualpage()** function is used to display pages other than 0; for example, to display video page 1 you would set *page* to 1. The prototype for **setvisualpage()** is in **graphics.h**.

Related function: **setactivepage()**.

#include <conio.h>
void textattr(int attr)

The **textattr()** function sets both the foreground and background colors in a text screen at one time. The value of *attribute* represents an encoded form of the color information, as shown here:

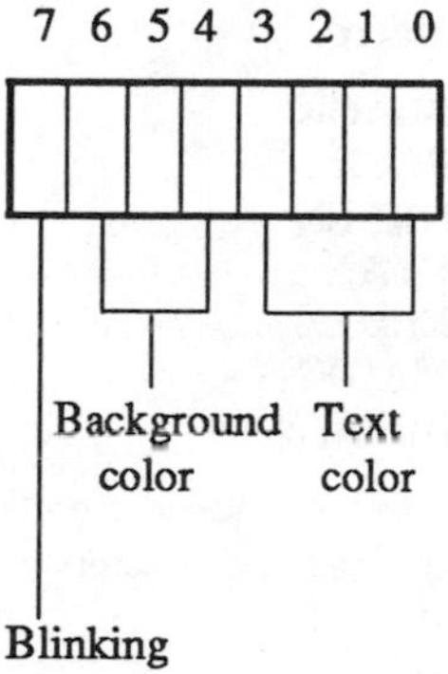

If bit 7 is set, the text will blink. Bits 6 through 4 determine the background color. Bits 3 through 0 set the color for the text. The easiest way to encode the background color into the attribute byte is to multiply the number of the color you desire by 16 and then OR that with the text color. For example, to create a green background with blue text you would use **GREEN * 16 | BLUE.** To cause the text to blink, OR the text color, background color, and BLINK (128) together.

Related functions: **textbackground(), textcolor().**

#include <conio.h>
void textbackground(int color)

The **textbackground()** function sets the background color of a text screen. A call to **textbackground()** only affects the background color of subsequent write operations. The valid values for *color* are shown here, along with their macro names (defined in **conio.h**):

Value	Macro
0	BLACK
1	BLUE
2	GREEN
3	CYAN
4	RED
5	MAGENTA
6	BROWN

The new background color affects text entered after the call to **textbackground()**; the background of characters currently on the screen are not affected.

Related function: **textcolor()**.

#include <conio.h>
void textcolor(int color)

The **textcolor()** function sets the color in which characters are displayed in a text screen. It may also be used to specify blinking characters. The valid values for *color*, along with their macro names (defined in **conio.h**), are shown here:

Value	Macro
0	BLACK
1	BLUE
2	GREEN
3	CYAN
4	RED
5	MAGENTA
6	BROWN
7	LIGHTGRAY

Value	Macro
8	DARKGRAY
9	LIGHTBLUE
10	LIGHTGREEN
11	LIGHTCYAN
12	LIGHTRED
13	LIGHTMAGENTA
14	YELLOW
15	WHITE
128	BLINK

Only text entered after **textcolor()** has been executed will be affected; the color of characters on the screen are not changed by **textcolor()**.

Related function: **textattr()**.

#include <graphics.h>
int far textheight(char far *str)

The **textheight()** function returns the height, in pixels, of the string pointed to by *str* in relation to the current font and size. The prototype for **textheight()** is in **graphics.h**.

Related function: **textwidth()**.

#include <conio.h>
void textmode(int mode)

The **textmode()** function is used to change the video mode of a text screen. The *mode* argument must be one of the values shown in the following table. You may use either the integer value or the macro name (the macros are defined in **conio.h**).

Value	Macro	Description
0	BW40	40-column black and white
1	C40	40-column color
2	BW80	80-column black and white
3	C80	80-column color
7	MONO	80-column monochrome
-1	LASTMODE	Previous mode

After a call to **textmode()**, the screen is reset and all text screen attributes are returned to their default settings.

Related function: **gettextinfo()**.

#include <graphics.h>
int far textwidth(char far *str)

The **textwidth()** function returns the width, in pixels, of the string pointed to by *str* in relation to the current font and size.

Related function: **textheight()**.

#include <conio.h>
int wherex(void)
int wherey(void)

The **wherex()** and **wherey()** functions return the current x and y cursor coordinates, respectively. The coordinates are relative to the current text window.

Related function: **gotoxy()**.

#include <conio.h>
void window(int left, int top, int right, int bottom)

The **window()** function is used to create a rectangular text window whose upper-left and lower-right coordinates are specified by *left,top* and *right,bottom,* respectively. If any coordinate is invalid, **window()** takes no action. Once a call to **window()** has been successfully completed, all references to location coordinates are interpreted in relation to the window, not the screen.

Related function: **clrscr()**.

TIME, DATE, AND SYSTEM-RELATED FUNCTIONS

This section covers functions, defined by the proposed ANSI standard, that are operating-system sensitive. These include the time and date functions that use the operating system's time and date information.

Also discussed are functions that allow direct operating-system interfacing, none of which are defined by the proposed ANSI standard, because each operating environment is different. However, Turbo C provides extensive DOS and BIOS interfacing functions that allow you to wring every ounce of performance out of the computer.

The functions that deal with the system time and date require the header **time.h** for their prototypes. Also included in this header are two defined types. The type **time_t** is capable of representing the system time and date as a long integer; this is referred to as the *calendar time*. The structure type **tm** holds the date and time broken down into their elements. The **tm** structure is defined as

```
struct tm {
   int tm_sec;  /* seconds, 0-59 */
   int tm_min;  /* minutes, 0-59 */
   int tm_hour; /* hours, 0-23 */
   int tm_mday; /* day of the month, 1-31 */
   int tm_mon;  /* months since Jan, 0-11 */
   int tm_year; /* years from 1900 */
   int tm_wday; /* days since Sunday, 0-6 */
   int tm_yday; /* days since Jan 1, 0-365 */
   int tm_isdst /* Daylight Savings Time indicator */
}
```

The value of *tm_isdst* will be positive if Daylight Savings Time is in effect, 0 if it is not in effect, and negative if there is no information available. This form of the time and date is called the *broken-down time*.

Turbo C also includes some nonstandard time and date functions that bypass the normal time and date system and interface more closely with DOS. The functions use structures of either type **time** or **date**, which are defined in **dos.h**. Their declarations are shown here:

```
struct date {
   int da_year; /* year */
   char da_day; /* day of month */
   char da_mon; /* month, Jan=1 */
};
struct time {
   unsigned char ti_min;  /* minutes */
   unsigned char ti_hour; /* hours */
```

```
    unsigned char ti_hund; /* hundredths of seconds */
    unsigned char ti_sec;   /* seconds */
};
```

The DOS interfacing functions require the header **dos.h**. The **dos.h** file defines a union that corresponds to the registers of the 8088/86 CPU and is used by some of the system interfacing functions. This definition as the union of two structures allows each register to be accessed by either word or byte:

```
struct WORDREGS
            {
            unsigned int    ax, bx, cx, dx, si, di, cflag;
            };

struct BYTEREGS
            {
            unsigned char   al, ah, bl, bh, cl, ch, dl, dh;
            };

union   REGS   {
            struct  WORDREGS x;
            struct  BYTEREGS h;
};
```

Also defined in **dos.h** is the structure type **SREGS**, which is used by some functions to set the segment registers. It is defined as

```
struct SREGS   {
    unsigned int  es;
    unsigned int  cs;
    unsigned int  ss;
```

```
    unsigned int  ds;
};
```

Several of the functions described here interface directly to the ROM-BIOS, the lowest level of the operating system. These functions require the header **bios.h**. A few functions require other predefined structures, which will be described as needed.

#include <dos.h>
**int absread(int drive, int numsects,
        int sectnum, void *buf)**
**int abswrite(int drive, int numsects,
        int sectnum, void *buf)**

The **absread()** and **abswrite()** functions perform absolute disk read and write operations, respectively. They bypass the logical structure of the disk and ignore files or directories. Instead, they operate on the disk at the sector specified in *sectnum*. The drive is specified in *drive*, with drive A equal to 0. The number of sectors to read or write is specified in *numsects*, and the information is read into or from the region of memory pointed to by *buf*.

These functions return 0 on success; a nonzero value is returned on failure.

Related functions: **read()**, **fread()**, **write()**, **fwrite()**.

```
#include <time.h>
char *asctime(struct tm *ptr)
```

The **asctime()** function returns a pointer to a string, consisting of the information stored in the structure pointed to by *ptr* converted into the following form:

```
day month date hours:minutes:seconds year\n\0
```

Here is an example:

```
Wed Jun 19 12:05:34 1999
```

The structure pointer passed to **asctime()** is generally obtained from either **localtime()** or **gmtime()**. The buffer used by **asctime()** to hold the formatted output string is a statically allocated character array and is overwritten each time the function is called. If you wish to save the contents of the string, you must copy it elsewhere.

Related functions: **localtime()**, **gmtime()**, **time()**, **ctime()**.

```
#include <dos.h>
int bdos(int fnum, unsigned dx,
        unsigned al)
int bdosptr(int fnum, void *dsdx,
        unsigned al)
```

The **bdos()** function is used to access the DOS system call specified by *fnum*. First it places the values *dx* into the DX register and *al* into the AL register, and then it executes an INT 21H instruction.

If you will be passing a pointer argument to DOS, use the **bdosptr()** function instead of **bdos()**. For the tiny, small, and medium memory models, the two functions are operationally equivalent, but when larger memory models are used, 20-bit pointers are required. In this case, the pointer will be passed in DS:DX.

Both the **bdos()** and **bdosptr()** functions return the value of the AX register, which is used by DOS to return information.

Related functions: **intdos()**, **intdosx()**.

#include <bios.h>
int bioscom(int cmd, char byte, int port)

The **bioscom()** function is used to manipulate the RS232 asynchronus communication port specified in *port*. Its operation is determined by the value of *cmd*, which has the following values:

Value	**Meaning**
0	Initialize the port
1	Send a character
2	Receive a character
3	Return the port status

Before using the serial port, you will probably want to initialize it to a setting other than its default setting. To do this, call **bioscom()** with *cmd* equal to 0. The exact way the port will be set up is determined by the value of *byte*, which is encoded with the following initialization parameters:

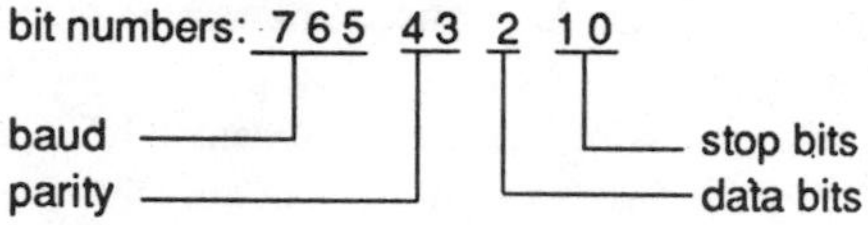

The baud is encoded as follows:

Baud	Bit Pattern
9600	1 1 1
4800	1 1 0
2400	1 0 1
1200	1 0 0
600	0 1 1
300	0 1 0
150	0 0 1
110	0 0 0

The parity bits are encoded as follows:

Parity	Bit Pattern
No parity	0 0 or 1 0
Odd	0 1
Even	1 1

The number of stop bits is determined by bit 2 of the serial port initialization byte. If it is 1, then two stop bits are used; otherwise, one stop bit is used. The number of data bits is set by the code in bits 1 and 0 of the initialization byte. Of the four possible bit patterns, only two are valid. If bits 1 and 0 contain the pattern 1 0, then seven data bits are used. If they contain 1 1, then eight data bits are used.

The return value of **bioscom()** is always a 16-bit quantity. The high-order byte is the status bits, which have these values:

Bit	Meaning
0	Data ready
1	Overrun error
2	Parity error
3	Framing error
4	Break-detect error
5	Transfer holding register empty
6	Transfer shift register empty
7	Time-out error

If *cmd* is set to 0, 1, or 3, then the low-order byte is encoded as shown here:

Bit	Meaning
0	Change in clear-to-send
1	Change in data-set-ready
2	Trailing-edge ring detector
3	Change in line signal
4	Clear-to-send
5	Data-set-ready
6	Ring indicator
7	Line signal detected

When *cmd* has a value of 2, the low-order byte contains the value received by the port. Most machines are not capable of using bioscom at speeds greater than 1200 baud because of the speed of the BIOS routines.

Related function: **bioskey()**.

#include <bios.h>
int bioskdisk(int cmd, int drive, int head, int track, int sector, int nsects, void *buf)

The **biosdisk()** function performs BIOS-level disk operations using interrupt 0x13. These operations ignore the logical structure of the disk, including files. All operations take place on sectors.

The affected drive is specified in *drive*, with 0 corresponding to A, 1 to B, and so on for floppy drives. The first fixed disk is drive 0x80, the second 0x81, and so on. The part of the disk that is operated on is specified in *head*, *track*, and *sector*. You should refer to the IBM PC *Technical Reference Manual* for details of the operation and options of the BIOS-level disk routines. Keep in mind that direct control of the disk requires thorough knowledge of both the hardware and DOS. It is best avoided except in unusual situations.

Related functions: **absread()**, **abswrite()**.

#include <bios.h>
int biosequip(void)

The **biosequip()** function returns a 16-bit value code for what equipment is in the computer. This value is encoded as shown here:

Bit	**Equipment**
0	Must boot from the floppy drive
1	80x87 math coprocessor installed

Bit	Equipment
2, 3	Motherboard RAM size
0 0: 16K	
0 1: 32K	
1 0: 48K	
1 1: 64K	
4, 5	Initial video mode
0 0: unused	
0 1: 40x25 BW, color adapter	
1 0: 80x25 BW, color adapter	
1 1: 80x25, monochrome adapter	
6, 7	Number of floppy drives
0 0: one	
0 1: two	
1 0: three	
1 1: four	
8	DMA chip installed
9, 10, 11	Number of serial ports
0 0 0: zero	
0 0 1: one	
0 1 0: two	
0 1 1: three	
1 0 0: four	
1 0 1: five	
1 1 0: six	
1 1 1: seven	
12	Game adapter installed
13	Serial printer installed (PCjr only)

Bit	**Equipment**
14, 15	Number of printers
0 0: zero	
0 1: one	
1 0: two	
1 1: three	

Related function: **bioscom()**.

#include <bios.h>
int bioskey(int cmd)

The **bioskey()** function performs direct keyboard operations, determined by the value of *cmd*.

If *cmd* is 0, **bioskey()** returns the next key struck on the keyboard. (It will wait until a key is pressed.) It returns a 16-bit quantity that consists of two different values. The low-order byte contains the ASCII character code if a normal key is pressed. It will contain 0 if a special key is struck, such as an arrow key or a function key. The high-order byte contains the scan code of the key, which corresponds to the position the key has on the keyboard.

If *cmd* is 1, **bioskey()** checks to see if a key has been pressed, It returns a nonzero value if a key has been pressed, and zero otherwise. When *cmd* is 2, the shift status is returned. The status of the various keys that shift are encoded into the low-order part of the return value, as shown here:

Bit	Meaning
0	RIGHT SHIFT pressed
1	LEFT SHIFT pressed
3	CTRL pressed
4	ALT pressed
5	Scroll Lock ON
6	Num Lock ON
7	Caps Lock ON
8	Insert ON

Related functions: **getche()**, **kbhit()**.

#include <bios.h>
► int biosmemory(void)

The **biosmemory()** function returns the amount of memory (in units of 1K) installed in the system.

Related function: **biosequip()**.

#include <bios.h>
► int biosprint(int cmd, int byte, int port)

The **biosprint()** function controls the printer port specified in *port*. If *port* is 0, LPT1 is used; if *port* is 1, LPT2 is accessed. The exact function performed is contingent on the value of *cmd*, as shown here:

Value	Meaning
0	Print the character in *byte*
1	Initialize the printer port
2	Return the status of the port

The printer port status is encoded into the low-order byte of the return value, as shown here:

Bit	Meaning
0	Time-out error
1	Unused
2	Unused
3	Unused
4	I/O error
5	Printer selected
6	Out-of-paper error
7	Acknowledge
8	Print NOT busy

Related function: **bioscom()**.

#include <bios.h>
long biostime(int cmd, long newtime)

The **biostime()** function reads or sets the BIOS clock. The BIOS clock ticks at a rate of about 18.2 ticks per second. Its value is 0 at midnight and increases until it is either reset at midnight again or manually set to some value. If *cmd* is 0, **biostime()** returns the current value of the timer. If *cmd* is 1, the timer is set to the value of *newtime*.

Related functions: **time()**, **ctime()**.

#include <dos.h>
struct country *country(int countrycode,struct country *countryptr)

The **country()** function sets several country-dependent items, such as the currency symbol and the way the date and time are displayed.

The *country* structure is defined as

```
struct country {
  int co_date;           /* date format */
  char co_curr[5];       /* currency symbol */
  char co_thsep[2];      /* thousand separator */
  char co_desep[2];      /* decimal separator */
  char co_dtsep[2];      /* date separator */
  char co_tmspe[2];      /* time separator */
  char co_currstyle;     /* currency style */
  char co_digits;        /* significant digits in currency */
  char co_time;          /* format of time */
  long co_case;          /* case map function */
  char so_dasep[2];      /* data separator */
  char co_fill[10];      /* filler */
};
```

If *countrycode* is set to 0, then the country-specific information is put in the structure pointed to by *countryptr*. The country function works with MS DOS version 3.0 or greater. If it is a nonzero value, the country-specific information is set to the value of the structure pointed to by *countryptr*.

The value of *co_date* determines the date format. If it is 0, U.S. style (month, day, year) format is used. If it is 1, the

European style (day, month, year) is used. If it is 2, the Japanese style (year, month, day) is used.

The way currency is displayed is determined by the value of *co_currstyle,* which has the following legal values:

Value	Meaning
0	Currency symbol immediately precedes the value
1	Currency symbol immediately follows the value
2	Currency symbol precedes the value, with a space between the symbol and the value
3	Currency symbol follows the value, with a space between the symbol and the value

The function returns a pointer to the *countryptr* argument.

Related functions: **time.h, ctime()**.

#include <time.h>
char *ctime(long *time)

The **ctime()** function returns a pointer to a string of the form

```
day month date hours:minutes:seconds year\n\0
```

given a pointer to the calendar time. The calendar time is generally obtained through a call to **time()**. The **ctime()** function is equivalent to

```
asctime(localtime(time))
```

The buffer used by **ctime()** to hold the formatted output string is a statically allocated character array and is overwritten each time the function is called. If you wish to save the contents of the string, you must copy it elsewhere.

Related functions: **localtime()**, **gmtime()**, **time()**, **asctime()**.

#include <dos.h>
► void ctrlbrk(int (*fptr)(void))

The **ctrlbrk()** function is used to replace the control-break handler called by DOS when the CTRL-BREAK key combination is pressed. A CTRL-BREAK generates an interrupt 0x23.

Turbo C automatically replaces the old control-break handler when your program exits.

Related function: **geninterrupt()**.

#include <time.h>
► double difftime(time_t time2, time_t time1)

The **difftime()** function returns the difference, in seconds, between *time1* and *time2*.

Related functions: **localtime()**, **gmtime()**, **time()**, **asctime()**.

#include <dos.h>
► void disable(void)

The **disable()** function disables interrupts. The only interrupt that it allows is the NMI (nonmaskable interrupt). Use this function with care because many devices in the system use interrupts.

Related functions: **enable()**, **geninterrupt()**.

#include <dos.h>
int dosexterr(struct DOSERR *err)

The **dosexterr()** function fills the structure pointed to by *err* with extended error information when a DOS call fails. The **DOSERR** structure is defined like this:

```
struct DOSERR {
  int exterror; /* error code */
  int class;    /* class of error */
  char action   /* suggested action */
  char locus;   /* location of error */
};
```

For the proper interpretation of the information returned by DOS, refer to the *DOS Technical Reference Manual*.

Related function: **ferror()**.

#include <dos.h>
long dostounix(struct date *d, struct time *t)

The **dostounix()** function returns the system time as returned by **gettime()** and **getdate()** into a form compatible with the UNIX-style time format (also the ANSI standard format).

Related functions: **unixtodos()**, **ctime()**, **time()**.

```
#include <dos.h>
void endable(void)
```

The **enable()** function enables interrupts.

Related functions: **disable()**, **geninterrupt()**.

```
#include <dos.h>
unsigned FP_OFF(void far *ptr)
unsigned FP_SEG(void far *ptr)
```

The **FP_OFF()** and **FP_SEG()** functions return the offset and the segment portions of the **far** pointer *ptr*, respectively.

Related function: **MK_FP()**.

```
#include <dos.h>
void geninterrupt(int intr)
```

The **geninterrupt()** function generates a software interrupt. The number of the interrupt generated is determined by the value of *intr*.

Related functions: **enable()**, **disable()**.

```
#include <dos.h>
int getcbrk(void)
```

The **getcbrk()** function returns 0 if extended control-break checking is off and 1 if extended control-break checking is on. When extended control-break checking is off, the only time DOS checks to see if the CTRL-BREAK key combination has been pressed is when console, printer, or auxiliary communication devices are performing I/O operations. When the extended checking is on, the CTRL-BREAK combination is checked for by each DOS call.

Related function: **setcbrk()**.

#include <dos.h>
void getdate(struct date *d)
void gettime(struct time *t)

The **getdate()** function fills the **date()** structure pointed to by *d* with the DOS form of the current system date. The **gettime()** function fills the **time()** structure pointed to by *t* with the DOS form of the current system time.

Related functions: **settime()**, **setdate()**.

#include <dos.h>
void getdfree(int drive, struct dfree *dfptr)

The **getdfree()** function returns the amount of free disk space in the structure pointed to by *dfptr* for the drive specified by *drive*. The drives are numbered from 1 for drive A and so on. You can specify the default drive by giving *dfree* the value 0. The *dfree* structure is defined as

```
struct dfree {
  unsigned df_avail;  /* unused clusters */
  unsigned df_total;  /* total number of clusters */
  unsigned df_bsec;   /* number of bytes per cluster */
  unsigned df_sclus;  /* number of sectors per cluster */
};
```

If an error occurs, the *df_sclus* field is set to -1.

Related function: **getfat()**.

#include <dos.h>
char far *getdta(void)

The **getdta()** function returns a pointer to the disk transfer address. A **far** pointer is returned because you cannot assume, in all circumstances, that the disk transfer address will be located within the data segment of your program.

Related function: **setdta()**.

#include <dos.h>
void getfat(int drive, struct fatinfo *fptr)
void getfatd(struct fatinfo *fptr)

The **getfat()** function returns various information about the disk in *drive* gathered from that drive's file allocation table (FAT). If the value of *drive* is 0, the default drive is used. Otherwise, use 1 for drive A, 2 for B, and so on. The structure pointed to by *fptr* is loaded with the information from the FAT. The structure *fatinfo* is defined as

```
struct fatinfo {
  char fi_sclus; /* number of sectors per cluster */
  char fi_fatid; /* FAT ID */
  int fi_nclus;  /* total number of clusters */
  int fi_bysec;  /* number of bytes per sector */
{;
```

The **getfatd()** function is the same as **getfat()** except the default drive is always used.

Related function: **getdfree()**.

B. Dalton Bookseller Friendswood, TX
22 767.01.10 11/18/89 20.56 427

0078813816		5.95
0822006456		3.75
	SUBTOTAL	9.70
	SALES TAX	0.78
	TOTAL	10.48
	CASH	10.48

---------------- THANK YOU ----------------

B. Dalton Bookseller Friendswood, TX
22 767.01.10 11/18/89 20.56 + 427

0078813818		5.95
0822006456		3.75
	SUBTOTAL	9.70
	SALES TAX	0.78
	TOTAL	10.48
	CASH	10.48

------------ THANK YOU ------------

#include <dos.h>
int getftime(int handle, struct ftime *ftptr)

The **getftime()** function returns the time and date of creation of the file associated with *handle*. The information is loaded into the structure pointed to by *ftptr*. The bit-field structure *ftime* is defined as

```
struct ftime {
  unsigned ft_tsec: 5; /* seconds */
  unsigned ft_min: 6;  /* minutes */
  unsigned ft_hour: 5; /* hours */
  unsigned ft_day: 5;  /* days */
  unsigned ft_month: 4 /* month */
  unsigned ft_year: 7  /* year from 1980 */
};
```

The **getftime()** function returns 0 if successful. If an error occurs, -1 is returned and **errno** is set to either **EINVFNC** (invalid function number) or **EBADF** (bad file number).

Related function: **open()**.

#include <dos.h>
unsigned getpsp(void)

The **getpsp()** function returns the segment of the program segment prefix (PSP). This function only works with DOS version 3.0 or greater.

The PSP is also set in the global variable **_psp**, which may be used with versions of DOS greater than 2.0.

Related function: **biosdisk()**.

#include <dos.h>
void interrupt(*getvect(int intr))(void)

The **getvect()** function returns the address of the interrupt service routine associated with the interrupt specified in *intr*. This value is returned as a **far** pointer.

Related function: **setvect()**.

#include <dos.h>
int getverify(void)

The **getverify()** function returns the status of the DOS verify flag. When this flag is on, all disk writes are verified against the output buffer to ensure that the data is properly written. When the verify flag is off, no verification is performed and 0 is returned; otherwise, 1 is returned.

Related function: **setverify()**.

#include <time.h>
struct tm *gmtime(time_t time)

The **gmtime()** function returns a pointer to the broken-down form of *time* in the form of a **tm** structure. The time is represented in Greenwich mean time. The *time* value is obtained through a call to **time()**.

The structure used by **gmtime()** to hold the broken-down time is statically allocated and is overwritten each time the function is called. If you wish to save the contents of the structure, you must copy it elsewhere.

Related functions: **localtime()**, **time()**, **asctime()**.

#include <dos.h>
► void harderr(int (*int_handler)())
void hardresume(int code)
void hardretn(code)

The **harderr()** function allows you to replace the DOS default hardware error handler with one of your own. The function is called with the address of the function that will be the new error handling routine. It will be executed each time an interrupt 0x24 occurs.

Assuming the error handling function is called **err_handler()**, it must have the following prototype:

```
int err_handler(int errnum, int ax, int bp, int si);
```

Here, *errnum* is the DOS error code, and *ax, bp,* and *si* contain the values of the AX, BP, and SI registers. If *ax* is not negative, a disk error has occurred, in which case ANDing *ax* with interrupt 0xFF will yield the number of the drive that failed (drive A equals 1, and so on). If *ax* is negative, a device failed. You must consult a DOS technical reference guide for complete interpretation of the error codes. The *bp* and *si* registers contain the address of the device driver for the device that sustained the error.

There are two very important rules that you must follow when creating your own error handlers. First, the interrupt handler must not use any of Turbo C's standard or UNIX-like I/O functions. Attempting to use them in the handler will crash the computer. Second, you may use only DOS calls, number 1 through number 12.

The error interrupt handler can exit in one of two ways. First, the **hardresume()** function causes the handler to exit to

DOS, returning the value of *code*. Second, the handler can return to the program through a call to **hardretn()** with a return value of *code*. In either case, the value returned must be 0 for ignore, 1 for retry, or 2 for abort.

Related function: **geninterrupt()**.

#include <dos.h>
int inport(int port)
int intportb(int port)

The **inport()** function returns the word value read from the port specified in *port*. The **inportb()** function returns a byte read from the specified port. The **inport()** and **intportb()** functions are also a macro that is defined in dos.h.

Related functions: **outport()**, **outportb()**.

#include <dos.h>
int int86(int int_num, union REGS *in_regs, union REGS *out_regs)
int int86x(int int_num, union REGS *in_regs, union REGS *out_regs, struct SREGS *segregs)

The **int86()** function is used to execute a software interrupt specified by *int_num*. The contents of the union *in_regs* is copied into the registers of the processor, and then the proper interrupt is executed.

Upon return, the union *out_regs* will contain the values of the registers that the CPU has upon return from the interrupt. If the carry flag is set, an error has occurred. The value of the AX register is returned.

The **int86x()** function copies the values of *segregs->ds* into the DS register and *segregs->es* into the ES register. This allows programs compiled for the large data model to specify which segments to use during the interrupt.

Related functions: **intdos()**, **bdos()**.

```
#include <dos.h>
int intdos(union REGS *in_regs,
        union REGS *out_regs)
int intdosx(union REGS *in_regs,
        union REGS *out_regs,
        struct SREGS *segregs)
```

The **intdos()** function is used to access the DOS system call specified by the contents of the union pointed to by *in_regs*. It executes an INT 21H instruction, and the outcome of the operation is placed in the union pointed to by *out_regs*. The **intdos()** function returns the value of the AX register, which is used by DOS to return information. If the carry flag is set upon return, an error has occurred.

For **intdosx()**, the value of *segregs* specifies the DS and ES registers. This is used principally in programs compiled using the large data models.

Related functions: **bdos()**, **int86()**.

#include <dos.h>
► void intr(int intr_num, struct REGPACK *reg)

The **intr()** function executes the software interrupt specified by *intr_num*. It provides an alternative to the **int86()** function, but does not contain any expanded functionality.

The values of the registers in the structure pointed to by *reg* are copied into the CPU registers before the interrupt occurs. After the interrupt returns, the structure will contain the values of the register as set by the interrupt service routine. The *REGPACK* structure is defined as shown here:

```
struct REGPACK {
   unsigned r_as, r_bx, r_cx, r_dx;
   unsigned r_bp, r_si, r_di, r_ds, r_es;
   unsigned r_flags;
};
```

Any registers not used by the interrupt are ignored.

Related functions: **int86()**, **intdos()**.

#include <dos.h>
► void keep(int status, int size)

The **keep()** function exits an interrupt 0x31, which causes the current program to terminate, but stay resident. The value of *status* is returned to DOS as a return code. The size of the program that is to stay resident is specified in *size* paragraph. The rest of the memory is freed for use by DOS.

Related function: **geninterrupt()**.

#include <time.h>
struct tm *localtime(time_t *time)

The **localtime()** function returns a pointer to the broken-down form of *time* in the form of a **tm** structure. The time is represented in local time. The *time* value generally is obtained through a call to **time()**.

The structure used by **localtime()** to hold the broken-down time is statically allocated and is overwritten each time the function is called. If you wish to save the contents of the structure, you must copy it elsewhere.

Related functions: **gmtime()**, **time()**, **asctime()**.

#include <dos.h>
void far *MK_FP(unsigned seg, unsigned off)

The **MK_FP()** macro returns a **far** pointer given the segment *seg* and the offset *off*.

Related functions: **FP_OFF()**, **FP_SEG()**.

#include <dos.h>
void outport(int port, int word)
void outportb(int port, char byte)

The **outport()** function outputs the value of *word* to the port specified in *port*. The **outportb()** function outputs the specified byte to the specified port. The **outport()** and **outportb()** functions are also macros defined in dos.h.

Related functions: **inport()**, **inportb()**.

#include <dos.h>
char *parsfnm(char *fname, struct fcb *fcbptr, int option)

The **parsfnm()** function converts a filename contained in a string into the form required by the file control block and places it into the one pointed to by *fcbptr*. This function is frequently used with command line arguments. It uses DOS function 0x29. The *option* parameter is used to set the AL register prior to the call to DOS. Refer to a DOS programmer's manual for complete information on the 0x29 function. The *fcb* structure is defined as

```
struct fcb {
  char  fcb_drive;    /* 0 = default, 1 = A, 2 = B */
  char  fcb_name[8];  /* Filename */
  char  fcb_ext[3];   /* File extension */
  short fcb_curblk;   /* Current block number */
  short fcb_recsize;  /* Logical record size in bytes */
  long  fcb_filsize;  /* File size in bytes */
  short fcb_date;     /* Date file was last written */
  char  fcb_resv[10]; /* Reserved for DOS */
  char  fcb_currec;   /* Current record in block */
  long  fcb_random;   /* Random record number */
};
```

If the call to **parsfnm()** is successful, a pointer to the next byte after the filename is returned; when an error occurs, 0 is returned.

Related function: **fopen()**.

#include <dos.h>
int peek(int seg, unsigned offset)
char peekb(int seg, unsigned offset)
void poke(int seg, unsigned offset, int word)
void pokeb(int seg, unsigned offset, char byte)

The **peek()** function returns the 16-bit value at the location in memory pointed to by *seg:offset*. The **peekb()** function returns the 8-bit value at the location in memory pointed to by *seg:offset*. The **poke()** function stores the 16-bit value of *word* at the address pointed to by *seg:offset*, and the **pokeb()** function stores the 8-bit value of *byte* at the address pointed to by *seg:offset*.

Related functions: **FP_OFF(), FP_SEG(), MK_FP().**

#include <dos.h>
int randbrd(strcut fcb *fcbptr, int count)
int randbwr(strcut fcb *fcbptr, int count)

The **randbrd()** function reads *count* number of records into the memory at the current disk transfer address. The actual records read are determined by the values of the structure pointed to by *fcbptr*. The *fcb* structure is defined as

```
struct fcb {
  char  fcb_drive;    /* 0 = default, 1 = A, 2 = B */
  char  fcb_name[8];  /* Filename */
  char  fcb_ext[3];   /* File extension */
  short fcb_curblk;   /* Current block number */
  short fcb_recsize;  /* Logical record size in bytes */
```

```
    long  fcb_filsize;  /* File size in bytes */
    short fcb_date;     /* Date file was last written */
    char  fcb_resv[10]; /* Reserved for DOS */
    char  fcb_currec;   /* Current record in block */
    long  fcb_random;   /* Random record number */
};
```

The **randbrd()** function uses DOS function 0x27 to accomplish its operation. Refer to a DOS programmer's guide for details.

The **randbwr()** function writes *count* records to the file associated with the *fcb* structure pointed to by *fcbptr*. The **randbwr()** uses DOS function 0x28 to accomplish its operation. Refer to a DOS programmer's guide for details.

The following values are returned by the functions:

Value	Meaning
0	All records successfully transferred
1	EOF encountered but the last record is complete
2	Too many records
3	EOF encountered and the last record is incomplete

Related function: **parsfnm()**.

#include <dos.h>
► void segread(struct SREGS *sregs)

The **segread()** function copies the current values of the segment registers into the structure *SREGS* pointed to by *sregs*. This function is intended for use by the **intdosx()** and **int86x()** functions; refer to them for further information.

#include <dos.h>
void setdate(struct date *d)
void settime(struct time *t)

The **setdate()** function sets the DOS system date as specified in the structure pointed to by *d*, and the **settime()** function sets the DOS system time as specified in the structure pointed to by *t*.

Related functions: **gettime()**, **getdate()**.

#include <dos.h>
void setdta(char far *dta)

The **setdta()** function sets the disk transfer address to that specified by *dta*.

Related function: **getdta()**.

#include <dos.h>
void setvect(int intr, void interrupt(*isr)())

The **setvect()** function puts the address of the interrupt service routine *isr* into the vectored interrupt table at the location specified by *intr*.

Related function: **getvect()**.

#include <dos.h>
void setverify(int value)

The **setverify()** function sets the state of the DOS verify flag. When this flag is on, all disk writes are verified against the output buffer to ensure that the data was properly written. If the verify flag is off, no verification is performed.

To turn on the verify flag, call **setverify()** with *value* set to 1. Set *value* to 0 to turn it off.

Related function: **getverify()**.

#include <dos.h>
► void sleep(unsigned time)

The **sleep()** function suspends program execution for *time* number of seconds.

Related function: **time()**.

#include <time.h>
► time_t time(time_e *time)

The **time()** function returns the current calendar time of the system. It can be called either with a null pointer or with a pointer to a variable of type **time_t**. If the latter is used, then the argument will also be assigned the calendar time.

Related functions: **localtime()**, **gmtime()**, **asctime()**, **ctime()**.

#include <time.h>
► void tzset(void)

The **tzset()** function is included in Turbo C for UNIX compatibility but does nothing whatsoever.

#include <dos.h>
void unixtodos(time_t utime, struct date *d, struct time *t)

The **unixtodos()** function converts UNIX's time format into a DOS format. The UNIX and ANSI standard time formats are the same. The *utime* argument holds the UNIX time format. The structures pointed to by *d* and *t* are loaded with the corresponding DOS date and time.

Related function: **dostounix()**.

MISCELLANEOUS FUNCTIONS

The functions discussed in this section are all the standard functions that do not fit easily into any other category. They include various conversion, variable length argument processing, sorting, and other functions.

Many of the functions covered here require the use of the header **stdlib.h**. This header defines two types: **div_t** and **ldiv_t**, which are the types of the values returned by **div()** and **ldiv()**, respectively. These macros are also defined:

- **ERANGE**: The value assigned to **errno** if a range error occurs.
- **HUGE_VAL**: The largest value representable by the floating point routines.
- **RAND_MAX**: The maximum value that can be returned by the **rand()** function.

Different header files required by some functions will be discussed in the function descriptions.

#include <stdlib.h>
► void abort(void)

The **abort()** function causes immediate termination of a program. No files are flushed. The **abort()** function returns 0 to the calling process (usually the operating system).

A common use of **abort()** is to prevent a runaway program from closing active files.

Related function: **exit()**.

#include <stdlib.h>
► int abs(int num)

The **abs()** function returns the absolute value of the integer contained in *num*.

Related function: **labs()**.

#include <assert.h>
► void assert(int exp)

The **assert()** function, defined in the header **assert.h**, writes error information to **stderr** and then aborts program execution if the expression *exp* evaluates to 0. Otherwise, **assert()** does nothing. The message written is similar to this:

```
Assertion failed: file <file>, line <linenum>
```

It is not necessary to remove the **assert()** statements from the source code once a program is debugged, because if the macro **NDEBUG** is defined before including the assert.h header file, then the **assert()** macros will be ignored.

Related function: **abort()**.

#include <stdlib.h>
int atexit(atexit_t func)

The **atexit()** function establishes the function pointed to by *func* as the function to be called upon normal program termination. That is, at the end of a program run, the specified function will be called. The type **atexit_t** is defined in the file **stdlib.h**.

The **atexit()** function returns 0 if the function is registered as the termination function; otherwise, a nonzero value is returned.

Up to 32 termination functions may be established, and they will be called in the reverse order of their establishment; that is, the registration process builds a stack of functions.

Related functions: **exit()**, **abort()**.

#include <math.h>
double atof(const char *str)

The **atof()** function converts the string pointed to by *str* into a **double** value. The string must contain a valid floating point number. If this is not the case, the returned value is technically undefined and 0 is returned.

Related functions: **atoi()**, **atol()**.

#include <stdlib.h>
int atoi(const char *str)

The **atoi()** function converts the string pointed to by *str* into an **int** value. The string must contain a valid integer number. If this is not the case, the returned value is technically undefined and 0 is returned.

Related functions: **atof()**, **atol()**.

#include <stdlib.h>
long atol(const char *str)

The **atol()** function converts the string pointed to by *str* into a **long int** value. The string must contain a valid long integer number. If this is not the case, the returned value is technically undefined and 0 is returned.

Related functions: **atof()**, **atoi()**.

#include <stdlib.h>
void *bsearch(const void *key,
const void *base, int *num, int size,
int (*compare)(const void *, const void *))

The **bsearch()** function performs a binary search on the sorted array pointed to by *base* and returns a pointer to the first member that matches the key pointed to by *key*. The number of elements in the array is specified by *num*, and the size (in bytes) of each element is described by *size*.

The function pointed to by *compare* is used to compare an element of the array with the key. The form of the *compare* function must be

```
func_name(void *arg1, void *arg2)
```

It must return the following values:

- If *arg1* is less than *arg2*, it returns less than 0.
- If *arg1* is equal to *arg2*, it returns 0.
- If *arg1* is greater than *arg2*, it returns greater than 0.

The array must be sorted in ascending order, with the lowest address containing the lowest element. If the array does not contain the key, a null pointer is returned.

Related functions: **qsort()**, **lsearch()**.

#include <stdlib.h>
div_t div(int numer, int denom)

The **div()** function returns the quotient and the remainder of the operation *numer/denom*.

The structure type **div_t** is defined in **stdlib.h** and has these two fields:

```
int quot;  /* the quotient */
int rem;   /* the remainder */
```

Related function: **ldiv()**.

#include <stdlib.h>
char *ecvt(double value, int ndigit,
int *dec, int *sign)

The **ecvt()** function converts *value* into a string of *ndigits* in length. After the call, the value of the variable pointed to by *dec* will indicate the position of the decimal point. If the decimal point is to the left the number, then the number pointed to by *dec* will be negative. If the variable pointed to by *sign* is negative, the number is negative.

The **ecvt()** function returns a pointer to a static data area that holds the string representation of the number.

Related functions: **fcvt()**, **gcvt()**.

```
#include <process.h>
int execl(char *fname, char *arg0, ...,
        char *argN, NULL)
int execle(char *fname, char *arg0, ...,
        char *argN, NULL, char *envp[])
int execlp(char *fname, char *arg0, ...,
        char *argN, NULL)
int execlpe(char *fname, char *arg0, ...,
        char *argN, NULL, char *envp[])
int execv(char *fname, char *arg[])
int execve(char *fname, char *arg[],
        char *envp[])
int execp(char *fname, char *arg[])
int execpe(char *fname, char *arg[],
        char *envp[])
```

The **exec** group of functions is used to execute another program. This other program, called the *child process*, is loaded over the one that contains the **exec** call. The name of the file that contains the child program is pointed to by *fname*. The arguments to the child process, if any, are pointed to either individually by *arg0* through *argN* or by the array *arg[]*.If you pass an environment string, it must be pointed to by *envp[]*. (The arguments will be pointed to by **argv** in the child process.)

If no extension or period is part of the string pointed to by *fname*, then first a search is made for a file by that name. If that fails, the .EXE extension is added, and the search is tried again. If an extension is specified, then only an exact match will satisfy the search. Finally, if a period but no extension is present, then only the file specified by the left side of the filename is searched for.

The exact way the child process is executed depends on which version of **exec** you use. You can think of the **exec** functions as having different suffixes that determine operation. A suffix may consist of either one or two characters.

Those functions that have a "p" in the suffix will search for the child process in the directories specified by the DOS PATH command. If a "p" is not in the suffix, only the current and root directories are searched.

An "l" in the suffix specifies that the arguments to the child process will be passed individually. You will want to use this method when you know in advance how many arguments will be passed. Notice that the last argument must be **NULL**, which is defined in **stdio.h**.

A "v" in the suffix means that the arguments to the child process will be passed in an array. This is the way you must pass arguments when you do not know in advance how many there will be.

Finally, an "e" in the suffix specifies that one or more environmental strings will be passed to the child process. The **envp** paramenter is an array of string pointers. Each string pointed to by the array must have this form:

```
environment variable = value
```

The last pointer in the array must be **NULL**. If the first element in the array is **NULL**, the child process retains the same environment as the parent. It is important to remember that files open at the time of an **exec** call will also be open in the child process.

When successful, the **exec** functions return no value. Upon failure, they return -1, and **errno** is set to one of these values:

Macro	Meaning
E2BIG	Too many arguments
EACCES	Access to child process file denied
EMFILE	Too many open files
ENOENT	File not found
ENOEXEC	Exec format error
ENOMEM	Not enough free memory

Related function: **spawn()**.

```
#include <process.h>
void exit(int status)
void _exit(int status)
```

The **exit()** and **_exit()** functions cause immediate, normal termination of a program. The value of *status* is passed to the calling process, usually the operating system. By convention, if the value of *status* is 0, normal program termination is assumed. A nonzero value may be used to indicate an implementation-defined error.

The function **exit()** flushes and closes any open files; **_exit()** does not. Also, **exit()** calls any exit functions established by the **atexit()** function, and **_exit()** does not.

Related functions: **atexit()**, **abort()**.

```
#include <stdlib.h>
char *fcvt(double value, int ndigit, int *dec,
        int *sign)
```

The **fcvt()** function is the same as **ecvt()** except that the output is rounded into the FORTRAN-compatible F format.

The **fcvt()** function returns a pointer to a static data area that holds the string representation of the number.

Related functions: **ecvt()**, **gcvt()**.

#include <float.h>
void _fpreset(void)

The **_fpreset()** functon resets the floating point arithmetic system. You may need to reset the floating point routines after a **system()**, **exec()**, **spawn()**, or **signal()** function executes.

Related function: **_status87()**.

#include <stdlib.h>
char *gcvt(double value, int ndigit,
char *buf)

The **gcvt()** function converts *value* into a string of *ndigits* in length. The converted string output is stored in the array pointed to by *buf* in FORTRAN F format if possible; otherwise, in E format. A pointer to *buf* is returned.

Related functions: **fcvt()**, **ecvt()**.

#include <stdlib.h>
char *getenv(const char *name)

The **getenv()** function returns a pointer to environmental information associated with the string pointed to by *name* in the DOS environmental information table. The string returned must never be changed by the program. The environment of a program may include such things as path names and devices online.

If a call is made to **getenv()** with an argument that does not match any environment data, a null pointer is returned.

Related function: **system()**.

#include <stdlib.h>
char *itoa(int num, char *str, int radix)

The **itoa()** function converts the integer *num* into its string equivalent and places the result in the string pointed to by *str*. The base of the output string is determined by *radix*, which may be in the range from 2 through 36.

Related functions: **atoi()**, **sscanf()**.

#include <stdlib.h>
long labs(long num)

The **labs()** function returns the absolute value of the **long int** contained in *num*.

Related function: **abs()**.

#include <stdlib.h>
ldiv_t ldiv(long numer, long denom)

The **ldiv()** function returns the quotient and the remainder of the operation *numer/denom*.

The structure type *ldiv_t* is defined in **stdlib.h** and has these two fields:

```
int quot;  /* the quotient */
int rem;   /* the remainder */
```

Related function: **div()**.

#include <setjmp.h>
void longjmp(jmp_buf envbuf, int val)

The **longjmp()** instruction causes program execution to resume at the location of the last call to **setjmp()**. These two functions are Turbo C's way of providing for a jump between functions.

The **longjmp()** function operates by resetting the stack to that stored in *envbuf*, which must have been set by a prior call to **setjmp()**. This causes program execution to resume at the statement following the **setjmp()** invocation; that is, the computer is "tricked" into thinking that it never left the function that called **setjmp()**.

The buffer *evnbuf* is of type *jmp_buf*, which is defined in the header **setjmp.h**. The buffer must have been set through a call to **setjmp()** prior to calling **longjmp()**.

The value of *val* becomes the return value of **setjump()** and may be interrogated to determine where the long jump came from. The only value not allowed is 0.

It is important to understand that the **longjmp()** function must be called before the function that called **setjmp()** returns. If not, the result is technically undefined, and a crash will almost certainly occur.

The most common use of **longjmp()** is to return from a deeply nested set of routines when a catastrophic error occurs.

Related function: **setjmp()**.

#include <stdlib.h>
char *ltoa(long num, char *str, int radix)

The **ltoa()** function converts the long integer *num* into its string equivalent and places the result in the string pointed to by *str*. The base of the output string is determined by *radix*, which may generally be in the range from 2 through 36.

Related functions: **itoa()**, **sscanf()**.

#include <stdio.h>
▶ void perror(const char *str)

The **perror()** function maps the value of the global **errno** onto a string and writes that string to **stderr**. If the value of *str* is not null, then the string is written first, followed by a colon and then the proper error message.

Related function: **ferror()**.

#include <stdlib.h>
▶ void qsort(void *base, size_t num, size_t size, int (*compare) (const void *, const void *))

The **qsort()** function sorts the array pointed to by *base* using a quicksort, which is generally considered to be the best general-purpose sorting algorithm. Upon termination, the array will be sorted. The number of elements in the array is specified by *num*, and the size (in bytes) of each element is described by *size*.

The function pointed to by *compare* is used to compare an element of the array with the key. The form of the *compare* function is

```
int func_name(const void *arg1, const void *arg2)
```

It must return the following values:

- If *arg1* is less than *arg2*, it returns less than 0.
- If *arg1* is equal to *arg2*, it returns 0.
- If *arg1* is greater than *arg2*, it returns greater than 0.

The array is sorted into ascending order, with the lowest address containing the lowest element.

Related function: **bsearch()**.

#include <stdlib.h>
int rand(void)
int random(int num)
void randomize(void)

The **rand()** function generates a sequence of pseudo-random numbers. Each time it is called, an integer between 0 and **RAND_MAX** is returned.

The **random()** function returns a pseudo-random integer in the range from 0 through *num-1*.

The **randomize()** function initializes the random number generator to some arbitrary value based on the system clock.

Related function: **srand()**.

#include <setjmp.h>
int setjmp(jmp_buf envbuf)

The **setjmp()** function saves the contents of the system stack in the buffer *envbuf* for later use by **longjmp()**.

The **setjmp()** function returns 0 upon invocation. However, a **longjmp()** passes an argument to **setjmp()** when it executes, and it is this value (always nonzero) that will appear to be the value of **setjmp()** after a call to **longjmp()**.

Related function: **longjmp()**.

```
#include <process.h>
int spawnl(int mode, char *fname,
        char *arg0, ..., char *argN, NULL)
int spawnle(int mode, char *fname,
        char *arg0, ..., char *argN, NULL,
        char *envp[])
int spawnlp(int mode, char *fname, char
        *arg0, ..., char *argN, NULL)
int spawnlpe(int mode, char *fname,
        char *arg0, ..., char *argN, NULL,
        char *envp[])
int spawnv(int mode, char *fname, char
        *arg[])
int spawnve(int mode, char *fname,
        char *arg[], char *envp[])
int spawnp(int mode, char *fname,
        char *arg[])
int spawnpe(int mode, char *fname,
        char *arg[], char *envp[])
```

The **spawn** group of functions is used to execute another program, the child process, which does not necessarily replace the parent program (unlike the child process executed by the **exec** group of functions). The name of the file that contains the child process is pointed to by *fname*. The arguments to the child process, if any, are either pointed to individually by *arg0* through *argN* or pointed to by the array *arg[]*. If you pass an environment string, it must be pointed to by *envp*.

(The arguments will be pointed to by **argv** in the child process.)

The *mode* parameter determines how the child process will be executed. It can have one of these three values (defined in **process.h**):

Macro	**Execution Mode**
P_WAIT	Suspends parent process until the child has finished executing
P_NOWAIT	Executes both the parent and the child concurrently (not implemented in Turbo C)
P_OVERLAY	Replaces the parent process in memory

Since currently the **P_NOWAIT** option is unavailable, you will almost always use **P_WAIT** as a value for *mode*. (If you want to replace the parent program, you are better off using the **exec** functions.) If the **P_WAIT** option is used, when the child process terminates, the parent process is resumed at the line after the call to **spawn**.

If no extension or period is part of the string pointed to by *fname*, then first a search is made for a file by that name. If that fails, the .EXE extension is added and the search is tried again. If an extension is specified, then only an exact match will satisfy the search. Finally, if a period but no extension is present, then only the file specified by the left side of the filename is searched for.

The exact way the child process is executed depends on which version of **spawn** you use. You can think of the **spawn** functions as having different suffixes that determine operation. A suffix may consist of either one or two characters.

Those functions that have a "p" in the suffix will search for the child process in the directories specified by the DOS PATH command. If a "p" is not in the suffix, only the current and root directories are searched.

An "l" in the suffix specifies that the arguments to the child process will be passed individually. You will want to use this method when you know in advance how many arguments will be passed. Notice that the last argument must be **NULL**, which is defined in **stdio.h**.

A "v" in the suffix means that the arguments to the child process will be passed in an array. This is the way you must pass arguments when you do not know in advance how many there will be.

Finally, an "e" in the suffix specifies that one or more environmental strings will be passed to the child process. The **envp()** parameter is an array of string pointers. Each string pointed to by the array must have this form:

```
environment variable = value
```

The last pointer in the array must be **NULL**. If the first element in the array is **NULL**, the child process retains the same environment as the parent.

It is important to remember that files open at the time of a **spawn** call will also be open in the child process.

When successful, the **spawn** functions return no value. Upon failure, they return -1, and **errno** is set to one of these values:

Macro	Meaning
EINUAL	Bad argument
E2BIG	Too many arguments
ENOENT	File not found
ENOEXEC	Spawn format error
ENOMEM	Not enough free memory

A spawned process can spawn another process. The level of nested spawns is limited by the amount of available RAM and the size of the programs.

Related function: **exec()**.

#include <stdlib.h>
void srand(unsigned seed)

The **srand()** function is used to set a starting point for the sequence generated by **rand()**; the **rand()** function returns pseudo-random numbers.

Related function: **rand()**.

#include <stdlib.h>
double strtod(const char *start, char **end)

The **strtod()** function converts the string representation of a number stored in the string pointed to by *start* into a **double** and returns the result.

The **strtod()** function starts by stripping any white space in the string pointed to by *start*. Next, each character that comprises the number is read. Any character that cannot be part of a floating point number will cause this process to stop. This includes white space, punctuation (other than periods), and characters other than "E" or "e." Finally, *end* is set to point to the remainder, if any, of the original string.

Related function: **atof()**.

#include <stdlib.h>
long strtol(const char *start, char **end, int radix)

The **strtol()** function converts the string representation of a number stored in the string pointed to by *start* into a **long** and returns the result. The base of the number is determined by *radix*. If *radix* is 0, the base is determined by rules that govern constant specification. If *radix* is a nonzero value, then it must be in the range from 2 through 36.

The **strtol()** function starts by stripping any white space in the string pointed to by *start*. Next, each character that comprises the number is read. Any character that cannot be part of a long integer number will cause this process to stop. This includes white space, punctuation, and characters. Finally, *end* is set to point to the remainder, if any, of the original string.

Related function: **atol()**.

#include <stdlib.h>
unsigned long strtoul(const char *start, char **end, int radix)

The **strtoul()** function converts the string representation of a number stored in the string pointed to by *start* into an **unsigned long int** and returns the result. The base of the number is determined by *radix*. If *radix* is 0, the base is determined by rules that govern constant specification. If *radix* is a non-zero value, then it must be in the range from 2 through 36.

The **strtoul()** function starts by stripping any white space in the string pointed to by *start*. Next, each character that comprises the number is read. Any character that cannot be part of an unsigned long integer number will cause this process to stop. This includes white space, punctuation, and characters. Finally, *end* is set to point to the remainder, if any, of the original string.

Related function: **strtol()**.

#include <stdlib.h>
int system(const char *str)

The **system()** function passes the string pointed to by *str* as a command to the DOS command processor. The function returns the exit code returned by the command processor.

Related function: **exit()**.

#include <stdarg.h>
void va_arg(va_list argptr, last_parm)
void va_end(va_list argptr)
va_arg(va_list argptr, type)

The **va_arg()**, **va_start()**, and **va_end()** macros work together to allow a variable number of arguments to be passed to a function. The most common example of a function that takes a variable number of arguments is **printf()**. The type *va_list* is defined by **stdarg.h**.

The general procedure for creating a function that can take a variable number of arguments is as follows. The function must have at least one known parameter, but may have more, prior to the variable parameter list. The rightmost known parameter is called the *last_parm*. Before any of the variable length parameters may be accessed, the argument pointer *argptr* must be initialized through a call to **va_start()**. After that, parameters are returned through calls to **va_arg()**, with *type* being the type of the next parameter. Finally, once all the parameters have been read and prior to returning from the function, a call to **va_end()** must be made to ensure that the stack is properly restored. If **va_end()** is not called, a program crash is very likely.

Related function: **vprintf()**.